OBSERVATIONS
ON THE
WESTERN PARTS OF ENGLAND

by
William Gilpin

New Introduction
by
Sutherland Lyall

THE RICHMOND PUBLISHING CO. LTD. 1973

Republished in 1973 by The Richmond Publishing Co. Ltd.
Orchard Road, Richmond, Surrey, England.

SBN 85546 182 9

Reprinted in Great Britain by Kingprint Limited
Richmond, Surrey.

THE WESTERN TOUR

by

Sutherland Lyall

The *Western Tour* (1798) was the last to be published during Gilpin's lifetime. The book would not have appeared until after 1804 had he not been persuaded that his free parish school at Boldre, which he financed from his picturesque sales, would benefit more from immediate rather than posthumous publication. The plates were by Samuel Alken on whose skill in aquatint Gilpin had increasingly relied as second and later editions of the *Tours* began to be published, and who was responsible for the execution of the plates in books from the *Lakes Tour* onwards. After 1796 when Blamire, Gilpin's publisher, failed, his picturesque texts including the *Western Tour* were all published by Cadell and Davies, who by 1808 had brought out a second edition of this book.

On his western tour Gilpin journied from London via Winchester, Salisbury, Wells and Bridgwater, as far into Cornwall as Bodmin, beyond which he had been told there was little interesting scenery to be seen. At Plymouth he, and possibly his wife who is known to have accompanied him on a number of the journeys, engaged some sailors to row them up the Tamar as far as Calstock before pressing on to Exeter and thence along the south coast with one detour to the Isle of Wight, to London.

On the way he visited Fonthill House where he found 'what is wanting in taste, is made up in finery. Never house was so bedecked with all the pride of upholstery.'; he felt he was insufficiently repaid for going so far out of his way to Lord Fortescue's at Castlehill in Devon; about Wilton Longleat and Fonthill he was lukewarm, reserving his enthusiasm about the works of man for the ruins of Glastonbury Abbey and this because Nature had decayed it into picturesqueness. In discussing picturesque beauty he said 'Neither grounds laid out by art, nor improved by agriculture, are of this kind.' And his greatest pleasure on this tour was the scene of the sun setting over the hills as he approached Wells 'The whole together invited the pencil, without soliciting the imagination. But it was a transitory scene. As we stood gazing at it, the sun sunk below the cloud, and being stripped of its splendour by the haziness of the atmosphere, fell, like a ball of fire, into the horizon; and the whole radiant vision faded away.'

Quite apart from the unusually lyrical quality of the whole description, it is of interest in that it contains more or less all the elements of picturesque beauty: the characteristically English haze which permeated the scene, the ruddy glow, which like a watercolour wash harmoniously united the elements, a boldly projecting hill acting as a side screen which framed the view of the towers of Wells beyond, all contrasting with the heavily shadowed foreground. Although picturesque beauty was fundamentally grounded in the appearance of Nature, as Gilpin frequently pointed out the most difficult thing was to get Nature to compose herself well: here she had.

Gilpin published nothing more during his lifetime. As far as picturesque theory was concerned there was no need to. Knight, Price and Repton had already begun their long public dialogue about the picturesque by the end of 1794, arguing not so much for gently improving nature to make a good picture, but for recreating nature in her own best composed image. For the picturesque tourist three more *Tours* were waiting. Their function was more to confirm in yet other parts of England the validity of Gilpin's mode of vision. By the first decade of the nineteenth century a flood of picturesque guides had begun to appear, the romantic poets had taken Gilpin's visual approach and turned it into a poetic one and the fashion for touring was well established. With this book the great work was done.

(ii)

NOTES

The plates throughout have been printed by offset photo – lithography.

A general introduction to William Gilpin and the Picturesque contributed by Sutherland Lyall accompanies the reprint of William Gilpin's *Wye Tour* (Richmond Publishing, 1973)

OBSERVATIONS

ON THE

WESTERN PARTS OF ENGLAND,

RELATIVE CHIEFLY TO

PICTURESQUE BEAUTY.

TO WHICH ARE ADDED,

A FEW REMARKS ON THE PICTURESQUE BEAUTIES OF THE ISLE OF WIGHT.

———

By WILLIAM GILPIN, M. A.

PREBENDARY OF SALISBURY; AND VICAR OF BOLDRE IN
NEW FOREST, NEAR LYMINGTON.

———

LONDON:

PRINTED FOR T. CADELL JUN. AND W. DAVIES, STRAND.
1798.

TO THE

RIGHT HONOURABLE

HENRY ADDINGTON,

SPEAKER OF THE HOUSE OF COMMONS.

———————————

DEAR SIR,

THOUGH your inquiries and pur-
ſuits have always been of a much
higher nature than the ſubject of theſe
papers, yet I take the liberty of pre-
ſenting them to you, as I am perſuaded
you do not diſapprove in others, what
the rigid economy of your own time
will not ſuffer you to purſue with much
attention yourſelf.

My book would gladly, however,
ſtill offer itſelf to your notice, from
ſome little perſonal affinity. It de-
ſcribes a country, through which you

have

have often travelled; and in which your property chiefly lies.

But if this plea have lefs weight, it hath one more, from whieh it hath a better hope of procuring a favourable reception. The profits of it are intended to lay the foundation of a little fund, which you, my dear Sir, and a few other kind friends, have obligingly engaged to countenance at fome future period.

As to the book itfelf, it has lain by me thefe twenty years, in which time it ought to have gained—and I hope it has gained—fome little advantage. One advantage is, that I have had opportunities of adorning feveral of the fcenes it defcribes, with contrafts taken from other countries, which have occafionally fallen in my way. It was always a particular amufement to my-

felf,

felf, and I hope it may be alfo to others, to fee how *varioufly* Nature works up the *fame modes* of fcenery, in different parts of the world.

At the fame time, fo long a date hath occafioned fome little anachronifms. I met with a few improvements in different places, of later date than the body of the work itfelf. Thefe indeed I might have inferted in notes; but I thought the occafion did not require much chronological exactnefs, and therefore blended them with the text.

After all, my dear Sir, to tell you the plain truth, in my addrefs to you, I confider my book only as a vehicle. The fact is, I had the vanity to wifh it known, that I could call one of the moft amiable and refpectable men I am acquainted with, my friend: and I hope you will excufe my not commu-

a 3   nicating

nicating to you this piece of vanity, as I had determined to indulge what I feared you might wifh to reprefs.

I beg, dear Sir, you will believe me to be, with the trueft efteem, refpect, and affection,

Your moft obedient, and

obliged humble fervant,

WILL. GILPIN.

Vicar's-hill,
April 23, 1798.

TABLE

OF

CONTENTS.

S E C T. XX.—P. 196.

S E C T. XXI.—P. 203.

S E C T. XXII.—P. 215.

S E C T. XXIII.—P. 220.

Berry-Pomeroy-caftle —Well at Brixham —Torbay—
Tor-abbey—Views about Teign-mouth—Mouth of the
Ex—Obftruction in the Ex between the Sea and Exeter—Views about the Mouth of the Sid—Valley of
the Sid from Honiton.

SECT. XXIX.—P. 269.

Vale of Honiton—Mofes's picturefque Defcription of Lot
entering Zoar—Rubens's Picture of Lot's Flight at Blen-
heim—Richnefs of the Country—Beauty of the Cattle—Axminfter—Different Kinds of Carpets—Turkey
—Britifh---Perfian.

SECT. XXX.—P. 274.

Ford abbey—In its ancient picturefque State—In its prefent improved and deformed State—Story of Mr.
Courtenay in a Storm at Sea.

SECT. XXXI.—P. 280.

Country from Axminfter to Bridport---From Bridport to
Dorchefter—Flocks of Sheep—A repofing Flock more
picturefque than a feeding one—Scenery of Duft—A
picturefque Reprefentation of this Kind in Xenophon's
Anabafis—Roman Antiquities —Amphitheatre —Maiden-caftle—Milton-abbey.

SECT. XXXII.—P. 290.

Blandford—Eaftbury—Brianfton—Badbury-ring—Downs
—Winborn—Ethelred's Tomb—Country about Pool —
Corff-caftle—Remarks of Lord Burleigh on the Coaft.
— Pool—Art of painting fmall Figures—Country be-
tween Pool and Chriftchurch.

LIST of the PLATES.

———

View

OBSERV.

OBSERVATIONS

ON THE

WESTERN PARTS OF ENGLAND.

―――――――

SECT. I.

OUR road led us firſt to Epſom through
Nonſuch-park. The very veſtiges of
the ſplendid palace and ſumptuous gardens of
Nonſuch, where Henry VIII. and Elizabeth
held their royal revelries, cannot now be
traced; except here and there, in the form of
a canal, or a terrace. Impreſſions made upon
the *ground itſelf*, are commonly more laſting
than any of the *works of art*, which are conſtructed on its ſurface. They are generally
more enormous; and the materials of no value.
Thus we have numberleſs tumuli---intrench-
ments—mounds—and ditches, of Roman and
Saxon conſtruction, which will probably ſee
as many ages as they have already ſeen: while

B   the

the architectural remains of those nations are either gone, or falling faſt into ruin. The ruin however of Nonſuch had an earlier date than happens to moſt great houſes. The prudent foreſight of the ducheſs of Cleveland, to whom Charles II. preſented it, was the cauſe of its ſpeedy diſſolution. She feared a reſumption, and pulling it in pieces, ſold the materials. It is ſomewhat remarkable that her father, Lord Francis Villiers, one of the handſomeſt men of his time, was killed, in the preceding reign, in a ſkirmiſh with a party of Cromwell's forces, on this very ſpot.

But though the building of Nonſuch was ſplendid, and the gardens ſumptuous beyond any of the royal houſes of that time, the ſituation has little merit. At this day, a ſituation is generally the firſt point attended to, as indeed it ought, in building a grand houſe; but formerly the very worſt ſituations ſeem to have been choſen; as if on purpoſe to ſhew the triumphs of art over nature. Indeed our anceſtors had little taſte for the beauties of nature; but conceived beauty to reſide chiefly in the expenſive conceits and extravagances of art; in which this palace particularly abounded. The body of the edifice formerly ſtood in a field,

field, acrofs the road, oppofite to a little farm,
now known by the name of the *Cherry-gar-
den*. If it had been carried a quarter of a mile
higher, where a detached building appendant
upon it, called the *banqueting-room*, formerly
ftood, its fituation would have been much better. It might have commanded a view over a
country, which is in fome parts pleafing.

Of the numerous appendages of this fumptuous pile, nothing remains but a houfe, now
modernized, which is faid to have been formerly
the habitation of Queen Elizabeth's maids of
honour. In the garden was a large chalk-pit,
containing about an acre of ground, which has
been planted, and formed into a pleafing little
fequeftered fcene by Mr. Whately, late fecre-
tary to the treafury, who wrote *Obfervations on
Modern Gardening*. His brother now poffeffes
that eftate, which was formerly the demefne of
the palace.

From Nonfuch we pafs through Ewel to
Epfom. Ewel is chiefly remarkable for a co-
pious fpring of limpid water, which arifing in
feveral parts of the village, forms itfelf into a

confi-

confiderable ftream. The baths collected from
it, are chill, and pure in a great degree. Epfom hath been defcribed by the pen of
Toland; who exercifed the powers of a wanton imagination with more innocence on this
fubject, than on many others. All that can
now be faid of it with truth (and it is *now*
much improved fince the days of Toland) is,
that it is a large pleafant village, built in the
form of a crefcent, in an open country ; and
that it contains a few elegant houfes. Of thefe
the moft remarkable is a houfe belonging to
the late Lord Baltimore; though it is now
neglected, and the park thrown into farms.

The chief recommendation of Epfom, is its
fituation on the fkirts of that open country,
called Banftead-downs, celebrated for hunting,
racing, cricket-matches, and mutton. Thefe
downs confift of beautiful fweeps of interfecting
grounds ; disfigured indeed here and there by
a chalky foil, but adorned with rich and very
picturefque diftances.

On thefe downs ftands a hunting-feat of
Lord Derby's, called the *Oaks*; which that no-
bleman

bleman brought into repute (for it was formerly an inn) by a very expensive summer-
evening entertainment, which he gave upon his
marriage. General Burgoyne celebrated both
the place and the occasion, in a small dramatic
piece, called the *Maid of the Oaks.*

Though this little villa is whimsical and singular, it has its beauty. It commands about
twenty acres, in an oblong form. In the centre stands the house, which is a kind of tower;
but yet unfinished. One half of the ground is
laid out in close walks, winding among *oaks,*
from whence the place has its name : the other
is a hanging lawn, interspersed with fir, flowering shrubs, and beeches. The oaks are ordinary ; and the firs scarcely yet half-grown;
but some of the beeches are of the grandest
form. The whole is surrounded by a sunk
fence ; and like an inchanted island in a desert,
appears a beautiful spot from every part of the
downs in its neighbourhood; and has itself a
grand view over them, as far as the towers of
London.

From Epsom we proceeded to Leatherhead,
skirting Lord Suffolk's park at Ashted : which
is

is a pleasant scene, including a great variety of ground, and some fine oaks and elms, within a walled circumference of about two miles. The house is not grand; but compact, and comfortable *.

* The house is now rebuilt. Sir Robert Howard, in Charles the Second's time, was the architect of the old house, which I thought, having often seen it, a very good one.

S E C T. II.

AT Leatherhead, inftead of continuing along the great road to Guilford, we turned fhort on the left, to take a view of Mr. Lock's houfe at Norbury-park; which ftands about half-way between that town and Dorking, on the banks of the Mole. Nothing in thefe parts is fo well worth a traveller's attention.

The beauties of the Mole itfelf deferve but little commendation. It is a lazy ftream; and finking into the ground in fome places, leaves its channel dry, in droughty feafons. Its banks, however, are beautiful in various parts; but in no part more fo than where Mr. Lock's woods and lawns rife loftily above them.

On entering the gate from the road, and paffing the Mole, we wind round the hill on the right towards the houfe, which ftands on the

fummit,

summit, removed from the sight, as we approach it; though from various parts of the country it is a conspicuous object.

Among other wood, which adorns this ascent, is a profusion of box. This plant grows here in full luxuriance, in its native uncultivated state; marking the road on the right with great beauty. A regular clipt box-wood hedge is an object of deformity: but growing wildly, as it does here, and winding irregularly, at different distances, along the road, it is very ornamental. The box itself also is a pleasing object: in winter it harmonizes with the ground; and, in summer, with the woods, which surround it. Box has a mellower, a more varied, and a more accommodating tint, than any ever-green. One other circumstance of advantage attends it. Almost every species of shrub, in a few years, outgrows its beauty. If the knife be not freely and frequently used, it becomes bare at the bottom; its branches dispart, and it rambles into a form too diffuse for its station. But box-wood long preserves its shape : and in the wild state in which we found it here, is far from regular; though its branches, which are never large, are close

and

and compact. I fhould, however, mention
holly, as having all the picturefque qualities of
box, except the variety of its tints. But in
the room of thefe it throws out its beautiful
clufters of coral berries, which have a pleafing
effect among its dark green polifhed leaves.
Like box it grows flowly, and alters leifurely.

After winding about a mile up the hill,
we arrive at the houfe, which is encircled
with groves of lofty, full-grown beech. The
back-front (if I may be allowed an awkward expreffion for want of a better) over-
hangs the fteep part of the hill; and commands, as you furvey it from the windows
of the houfe, a very grand vale; not like the
winding rocky vales of a mountainous country, but fuch as we fometimes find (though
rarely on fo ample a fcale) among the downy
hills of a chalky foil; though here the chalk
rarely offends. This vale is a flat area of cultivated ground, about five or fix miles in
length, and one in breadth. Sometimes indeed, though but rarely, it takes the form of a
lake or bay of the fea; which it exactly refembles when it happens to be overfpread by a
thick white fog, fuch a fog as from its gravity,
and

and the want of air to difturb it, finks to a level like water; and like water alfo defcribes the prominences of the vale around the bafes of the hills.

Generally indeed thefe heavy fogs are mifchievous, when they float over fea-marfhes, and other moift lands. A gentleman once fitted up a houfe near the coaft of Suffolk, which was often fubject to them. It ftood on a fmall eminence, in the midft of a rich woody vale; the whole furrounded by hills. Here the fogs would fometimes appear, in an autumnal evening, winding along the vale like a river, and fometimes like a lake; not with that indiftinct and vapourifh furface which fogs commonly affume, but flat, clear, and tranfparent; forming diftinctly all thofe little indentations which a water-line would have defcribed. Thefe beautiful exhibitions, though frequently prefented, never failed to pleafe. In the mean time the family were all feized with agues, fevers, and bilious diforders; and in three years found out, that thefe beautiful fogs were the caufe of their complaints. When the mafter of the fcene therefore had juft gotten his houfe and grounds completed, he was conftrained to leave them.

Norbury

Norbury park, however, is not fubject to
this beautiful mifchief. It is but rarely that
its vale is thus filled with a fleeping fog; and
when it is, the houfe ftands fo proudly above
it, that it defpifes its bad effects.

The fide-fcreen of this vale, on the right, as
you ftill furvey it from the windows, confifts
of a downy hill, marked with various large irregular channels, and planted with ancient oak
and beech. Through thefe woods, a walk is
conducted along its floping fide; from whence
you have defcending views into the vale below: fome of which feen through the fpreading arms of an oak or a beech, as through the
frame of a picture, have a pleafing effect.

The other fide-fcreen of the vale confifts of
that boaft of Surrey, the celebrated Box-hill;
fo called from the profufion of box which
flourifhes fpontaneoufly upon it. This hill
from its downy back and precipitous fides, exhibits great variety of pleafing views into the
lower parts of Surrey; and the higher parts
of the neighbouring counties. But we have here
only to do with it, as itfelf an object in a retiring fcene; in which it fills its ftation with
great beauty; difcovering its fhivering precipices, and downy hillocks, every where interfperfed

fperfed with the mellow verdure of box, which is here and there tinged, as box commonly is, with red and orange.

This hill, and the neighbouring hills, on which this beautiful plant flourifhes in fuch profufion, fhould be confidered as making a part of the natural hiftory of Britain. Affer, in his Life of Alfred the Great, tells us, that Berkfhire had its name from a wood, *ubi buxus abundantiffimè nafcitur.* No trace of any fuch wood now remains: nor is there perhaps a fingle bufh of indigenous box to be found in the whole country. All has been rooted up by the plough. If it were not therefore for the growth of box on the Surrey hills, whofe precipitous fides refufe cultivation, it might perhaps be doubted, whether box were a native of England. As to the common tradition of the country, that it was planted by an earl of Arundel, it is certainly fabulous: for there are court rolls ftill exifting, which mention *the box-wood on the hill,* before any fuch artificial plantation could have taken place *.

The

---

* Infignificant as this fhrub appears, it has been to its owner, Sir Henry Mildmay, a fource of confiderable profit. It is ufed chiefly in turning. But the fhips from the Levant brought fuch
quantities

The end-fcreen which fhuts in the beautiful vale juft'defcribed, confifts of the range of hills beyond Dorking; and the rifing grounds of Deepden; where in a clear day, a new houfe, built by the Duke of Norfolk, makes a confpicuous object. A little to the left of Dorking hills, the high grounds gradually falling, admit a diftant catch of the South downs, which overhang the fea.

Such is the fituation of this elegant villa; though, like all other fituations, it hath its favourable and unfavourable lights. It is feen to moft advantage in an evening. As the vale points almoft directly fouth from the houfe, the weft is on the right. In the evening therefore the woods of that fcreen are all in

---

quantities of it in ballaft, that the wood on the hill could not find a purchafer; and not having been cut in 65 years, was growing in many parts cankered. But the war having diminifhed the influx of it from the Mediterranean, feveral purchafers began to offer: and in the year 1795 Sir Henry put it up to auction; and fold it for the immenfe fum of twelve thoufand pounds. Box attains its full growth in about fifty years; in which time, if the foil be good, it will rife fifteen feet, nnd form a ftem of the thicknefs of a man's thigh. The depredations made on Box hill, in confequence of this fale, will not much injure its picturefque beauty; as it will be twelve years in cutting, which will give each portion a reafonable time to renew its beauty.

fhadow,

fhadow, which is flung in one vaft mafs over the bofom of the vale : while the fetting fun, having juft touched the tops of the trees, as its rays pafs over, throws a beautiful light on the guttered fides of Box-hill.

This view over the vale, (beautiful as it is,) is fubject, however, to inconvenience. Every houfe fhould, if poffible, overlook its *own domains*, as far at leaft as to remote diftance. All the intermediate fpace, in which objects are feen more diftinctly, may fuffer great injury from the caprice of different proprietors : and, in fact, this view has, in two or three inftances, fuffered injury from the interference of neighbours. This is indeed one reafon, among others, why noble palaces, with extenfive property on every fide, are moft adapted to thefe commanding fituations.

Norbury-houfe pretends only to comfort and convenience; except in the drawing room, which is an object of great curiofity. It is an oblong of 30 feet by 24. The walls are covered with a hard and durable ftucco, and are painted by Barret. The whole room reprefents a bower or arbour, admitting a *fictitious*
fky

sky through a large oval at the top, and covered at the angles with trellis-work, inter-
woven with honey-suckles, vines, clustering
grapes, and flowering creepers of various kinds.
The sides of the room are divided by slight
painted pilasters, appearing to support the trel-
lis roof; and open to four views. That towards the *south* is *real*, consisting of the vale
inclosed by Box-hill, and the hills of Norbury,
and Dorking, which hath been just described.
The other three are *artificial*. Two of them,
which are the two end-views, cover the whole
sides of the room from the ceiling to the
base.

The scene presented on the *west* wall, is
taken from the lakes of Cumberland. It is an
exact portrait of none of them; but a landscape formed from a collection of some of
the happiest circumstances which belong to
all. No real view could present so beautiful
and complete a picture. A large portion of
the lake, under a splendid calm, is spread before
the eye, surrounded by mountains perfectly
well shaped and stationed. Nature is not very
nice in the moulds in which she commonly
casts these enormous bodies; and as they have
various

various forms of beauty, fo have they of deformity ; but here we have fome of the moft pleafing fhapes culled out, and beautifully grouped. Woods are fcattered about every part, which give thefe fcenes a greater richnefs than nature hath given to any of the lakes in Cumberland. The fmaller ornaments alfo of buildings, figures, and boats are judicioufly introduced, and have a good effect. All this fcenery is contained in various removes of diftance ; for no part of the lake comes clofe to the eye. The near ground is compofed of bold rocks, and other rough furfaces, with which the banks of lakes commonly abound. Among thefe a wild torrent, varioufly broken, pours its waters under the furbafe of the room, which intercepts it. This torrent the painter has managed fo well, that its fpirit and brilliancy produce no lights which interfere with the calm refplendency of the lake, but rather contraft it.

In defcribing this noble landfcape, I have thus far confidered it chiefly as a *whole*. But all its *parts* are equally excellent. On the foreground particularly are two birch-trees, which are painted with great beauty. The roots, the bark, and the foliage, are all admirable.

The

The other grand landſcape occupies the *eaſt-
ern* wall of the room. It is, I think, inferior
to that on the *weſt*; yet it is a noble work.
The ſcene is ſylvan, and the objeɛts of courſe
leſs grand. The foreground, where we
admire particularly ſome beautiful trees, is
tumbled about in various forms; but in the
diſtance it ſinks into a rich flat country, through
which a ſluggiſh ſtream, winding its courſe, diſ-
charges itſelf into the ſea. The ſame obſervations might be made on this piɛture, which
were made on the other, with regard to compoſition, and the judicious management of the
ſeveral parts.

The *north* ſide of the room, oppoſite to the
windows, offers two more landſcapes; divided
by the breaſt of the chimney; which is
adorned with a pier-glaſs, let into the wall,
and covered thick with a frame-work of ho-
ney-ſuckles, vines, wild-roſes, and various
creepers in flower; all painted with great
beauty. Theſe two piɛtures on the *north* are
a continuation of the ſcene exhibited on the
weſtern wall, which they unite with the landſcape on the *eaſt*. Cluſtering vines, and wild
flowers, form a frame-work to all theſe beautiful piɛtures, both at the baſe, and along the

c   trellis-

trellis-work of the fides; fo as to give them the refemblance of being feen through the openings of the arbour.

With this *unity in the fubjects* of thefe land-fcapes, the *light* alfo, and other *particulars* co-incide. The *feafon* reprefented, is autumn. Every where round the room the year is in its wane. Each tree, and bufh, is touched with its autumnal hue. The *time of the day* is about an hour before the fun fets, which, after a rainy afternoon, is breaking out from the wa-tery clouds that are fcattered before a gentle breeze, in too high a region of the air to affect the furface of the lake. The rainy clouds, which are broken in the *weft*, hang heavy in the north; and give a dark lurid tint to the lake below. In the *north-eaft angle*, a ray of funfhine, breaking through the gloom, gilds a caftled cliff: but the clouds condenfing again, fall in a heavy, though a partial fhower on the landfcape in the eaft.

As the fun is reprefented fetting on the *weft-ern* fide of the room, it is *fuppofed* to illumine the feveral objects in *all* the pictures; and when the *natural hour* correfponds with the *hour reprefented*, there is a coincidence of *arti-ficial* and *natural* light. All the landfcape,

both

both within and without the room, appears illumined by the fame fun. The union too between the *natural* and *artificial* landfcape, is ftill farther affifted by a few ftraggling trees, which are planted before the windows, with a view to connect the picture with the *country*.

We dwell the longer on this curious and interefting room, as it is the only one of the kind perhaps in England. There is a room painted by the celebrated Gafper Pouffin, at the villa of Monte Dragone, near Rome, on a plan fomething like this; but Gafper has paid no attention to the union of the feveral *lights*, nor to the *characteriftic agreement* of the feveral views.

Added to the houfe is another grand room, full of much curiofity. It was built by Mr. Lock, as a painting room for the amufement of his eldeft fon, whofe genius, tafte, and knowledge in painting contend with our beft artifts. This room is adorned with a rich collection of ftatues, models, cafts, and bas-reliefs; all excellent in their kind: and an adjoining clofet is filled with heads, hands, feet, trunks, and other parts of the human body; fo that the whole together is a complete ftudy for a painter.

Among the cafts is a very fine one of the Venus of Medici. It is not common to fee fo

good

good a fubftitute of this figure. I have fometimes heard her *attitude* called in queftion. Inftead of that modeft demeanor, which is commonly afcribed to her, I have known her re-
proached for prudery, and theatrical affectation. We can, in truth, fay but little for her
moral character. Her *attitude*, however, I
think may be defended. The fculptor, I fuppofe, meant her to be viewed with her face towards you. In that pofition fhe makes the
moft elegant figure.

——Shrunk from herfelf,
With fancy blufhing,——

fhe received the fhot of the prophane eye that
furprifed her, as our modern heroes in duel-
ling receive a bullet, by inftantly drawing her
body into a profile. In both cafes nature
teaches the eafieft and moft commodious pofture.

But this collection, though it confift chiefly
of cafts, contains fome genuine antiques; particularly a Difcobolus, which is efteemed, I believe, the firft ftatue in England. It turns on
a pivot; and exhibits (what few ftatues are
able to exhibit) *on every fide* the jufteft proportions and the moft pleafing attitudes. But
what

what chiefly engages the attention in this ftatue, is its *expreffion*. It is a great beauty in
any figure to appear to have fome object in
view, which always gives animation to it. I
mean not that ftrong degree of action, which
the ancient mafters fometimes gave their
figures; as in the Laocoon, the fighting gladiator, and the Torfo, as far as we may judge of
that fragment from the fwelling of the mufcles.
Strong expreffion, no doubt, is highly beautiful,
when it is well executed. But I would here
only obferve the effect of fome *eafy action*, or
expreffion, in oppofition to *none at all*; as
in the Venus, the Belvidere Apollo, the liftening Slave, or the Farnefian Hercules, refting from one of his labours. All thefe gentle
modes of *action* or *expreffion* are certainly
much more beautiful than the uninterefting
vacancy of a conful ftanding erect in his robes.
Interefting he ftill may be, all I contend for is,
that fuch a ftatue is not *fo* interefting as if it
had fome object in view. The Difcobolus before us poffeffes this beauty in a diftinguifhed
manner. He has juft delivered his quoit; and
with an eager eye, and right arm ftill extended, is watching its fuccefs. The expanded
hand indicates, that the mind is yet in fuf-

c 3   pence.

pence *. His left hand holds another quoit; as, I fuppofe, each Difcobolus had two. It is probable, however, the ftatuary might have difpofed the left hand to more advantage, if he could have defcribed a quoit flying through the air. But he thought it neceffary in fome way to fhew in what mode of action his figure was engaged. Nature could not have told the ftory with more expreffion †.

As the ftatuary has generally a fingle figure only to manage, there is much artifice neceffary to fhew who he is; or, if he be employed, what he is about; and fometimes this is done very awkwardly. We might produce many inftances; but few perhaps more remarkable than M. Angelo's celebrated ftatue of Mofes. Unlefs the original greatly exceed any of the copies we have of it, it certainly deferves lefs praife than it has found. The face is incumbered with beard, and the body with drapery. But what I mean to remark at prefent is, the conceit with which the ftatuary has *charac-*

---

* The right hand, in this ftatue, is modern; but there is a repetition of this figure in the Mufæum Clementinum at Rome, which fhews, I am informed, the hand to have been well copied.

† This ftatue is now in the hands of Mr. Duncombe of Yorkfhire, who purchafed it of Mr. Lock.

terized

terized Mofes. Some fymbol was neceffary to
diftinguifh him from a Roman conful, fitting
in his curule chair. M. Angelo has given
him *horns*, by which he has turned him into a
fatyr. From whatever filly conceit the *idea* of
giving horns to the great Jewifh lawgiver
originally fprang, it is certainly abfurd in the
laft degree, to fee that *idea realized in marble*.
How much better might Mofes have been cha-
racterized fimply by his *rod*, and the *two tables
of the covenant* ; which latter, well managed,
might have made a broad contraft with the
drapery, while in part they might have been
covered with it.

Among fo many copies from the antique, it
is difficult to forbear remarking, that the hair
in fome of them is very awkwardly expreffed.
I have the Laocoon particularly in view. The
hair and beard of this ftatue have an uncommonly bad effect ; for as the face is turned
from the eye, the locks of hair, which are in
round curls, are confounded with the features
themfelves, prefenting a number of fmall cavi-
ties, whofe dark fhadows diminifh the effect of
thofe in the noftrils, mouth, and eyes, which
fhould give character and expreffion to the
face. It is a difficult thing, no doubt, to give

c 4 the

the eafe of hair to a block of marble: yet it
may be done in two ways. We have exam-
ples of both. The hair may be reprefented
very fhort, juft covering the head, approaching nearly to baldnefs, as we often fee it expreffed; or it may be reprefented in an eafy
flow. This is more difficult; yet we fometimes fee it well executed; and when it is fo,
it is certainly more beautiful than to exprefs
the hair in fmall ringlets, as it is in the Laocoon, and in many other antiques.

Before we leave this room, I cannot forbear
mentioning a head, which has a place there,
with hair of another kind. It plainly indeed
appeared allied neither to the Greek nor Roman models, among which it ftood, (for the
mouth was frightfully bad,) yet the *upper part*
of the face was executed with fimplicity, and
had fomething in it like tafte and beauty. On
inquiry we found it was a great curiofity, being
the workmanfhip of a native of Otaheite; and
feemed a convincing proof, that a love for the
imitative arts is innate. But what particularly
ftruck us in this head, was its being adorned
with *real hair*, which had a ftill worfe effect
than the beard of Laocoon. The mixture indeed of *reality* and *imitation*, is very difgufting;
and

and I doubt not would have appeared ſo on a little more knowledge and experience, to the ingenious ſculptor of the head himſelf. But we need not wonder at ſuch abſurdity in an artiſt of Otaheite, when we ſee among ourſelves ſo many ſhocking ſtatues, *painted after the life*; and vile waxen images with wigs and drapery ; things to ſhudder at, rather than to admire. The plain marble makes no pretence to any thing but *imitation*. It means not to put a *trick* upon us, by ſubſtituting itſelf for *real life*. But when we look at a waxen figure, arrayed in *real drapery*; yet with *rigid limbs*, and *glazed* and *motionleſs eyes*; that is, with every appearance of life about it but motion, in which the very eſſence of life conſiſts, we are ſhocked. The fact is, that when the *art of imitation* (applied to human life) is ſo perfect as to produce a *real*, though *momentary illuſion*, it preſents, by its *near approach to life*, an image of *death*. For the inſtant we perceive that a figure of this kind wants motion, we purſue it to the next ſtage, where motion ceaſes, which is *death*. A *repreſentation of a dead body* may be beautiful and pleaſing ; but a figure which preſents you with the appearance

ance of death, when you expected life, not only difgufts you by the fuddennefs of the tranfition; but alfo from the mind's having been even for a moment impofed on by fo paltry a trick.

From fuch effects, therefore, it feems to follow, that an *art calculated to pleafe by an imitation of life*, fhould, when applied to the human figure, though *neceffarily imperfect*, be made *intentionally* more fo ; left by too near an approach to *life*, it fhould fhock us with the idea of *death*.

Befides the fhock which thefe reprefentations give to the fenfes, they grofsly oppofe every idea of tafte. When we fee a ftuffed fkin in a Mufeum, we expect only an object of curiofity, and are fatisfied. But when a thing of this kind is fhewn as an *object of beauty*, it fets all tafte (which in natural objects feeks for nature) at defiance; and we confider a mummy, which aims at nothing but what it is, by many degrees the more refpectable figure.

As we leave this elegant manfion and defcend the hill, the views are more *picturefque* than thofe over the valley from the back-front. They confift of oblique fweeps of defcending

fore-

fore-grounds, every where well-wooded, and set off with remote diftances. This is the *fimpleft mode of landfcape*; but where the foreground and diftances are good, though there is a ftrong oppofition between them, they are not unpleafing.

A little to the right, as we defcend from the houfe, the beech-woods, confifting of lofty fullgrown trees, fweep down to the vale; though in lefs luxuriance, as they gradually defcend. When the defcent becomes precipitous, the channelled fides of the hill are, in many parts, bare of vegetation, and difcover the foil, which is not chalk, though of a chalky tendency, and rather grey than white. Patches of earth are mixed with thefe patches of barren foil, in which box-wood grows profufely; and here and there, where the foil allows, a luxuriant beech. Down this hill an Alpine road winds into the vale, and adds much to its beauty and character. It is ftill rendered more interefting by opening, in various parts, towards Box-hill; which prefents its flanks in thefe partial views, with a very mountain-like appearance. The whole fcene makes a good Alpine picture.

Our

Our remarks on this place fhould have been more curfory, if the plan of the whole, the fituation, and the embellifhments of it had not been all uncommon. Great houfes in general refemble each other fo nearly, that it is difficult to find among them any characteriftic features. Here the whole is new.

SECT. III.

FROM Norbury-park we returned to Leatherhead, and paſſed the Mole again in our
way to Guildford. The country on the left
conſiſts chiefly of open downs, which are rather narrow in this part, as they are drawing to
a point. They are interſperſed alſo with plots
of cultivation. As theſe downs are generally
high, we had, from many parts of them, a variety of beautiful diſtances on the right; not
ſo expanſive as thoſe from Banſtead-downs;
but more picturesque, as they are more within
the command of the eye. The great beauty of
ſuch ſcenes conſiſts in the richneſs of their
parts, in the removal of one diſtance beyond
another, diſcoverable chiefly by lengthened
gleams of light, and in the melting of the
whole into the horizon. If a diſtance be deprived of *any* of theſe characteriſtics, it is imperfect; but the laſt is moſt eſſentially neceſſary. A *hard edge* of diſtance checking the
view, (which is often the caſe when the diſtance is not remote,) is exceedingly diſguſting.

When

When the diftance indeed is bounded by mountains, it falls under other rules of picturefque
beauty.

Of the elevated fituation of thefe downs
much advantage hath been taken. Many elegant houfes are built upon the edge of them
for the fake of the various profpects they command. The whole country indeed from Leatherhead almoft to Guildford is thus richly
adorned. Two of the moft beautiful of thefe
villas, are thofe belonging to the late Admiral
Bofcawen and Lord Onflow. The latter is
efteemed one of the beft houfes in Surrey.
The grounds about it feem well difpofed; but
we only rode paft them.

A little to the left, near three parts of the
way to Guildford, we were directed to look
out, about half a mile from the road, for a
beautiful fcene called the *Sheep-leas*; confifting
of lawns, divided from each other by woody
copfes. We eafily found it; and were much
gratified with the appearance it prefented of a
fimple Arcadian retreat.

Few parts of this adorned tract of country
between Leatherhead and Guildford, (through a
fpace of about eleven miles,) can be called picturefque; yet from the variety it affords, it is

7   very

very amuſing. One of the great nuiſances of the landſcape here, as well as in other parts of the neighbourhood of London, is the formal manner which prevails of lopping trees, eſpecially elms. They are entirely deprived of the beautiful ramification of all their lateral branches, and you ſee them every where formed into mere poles, with a buſh at the top. *We* conſidered them only as objects of deformity: but the *ſkilful woodman*, I have heard, conſiders ſuch mutilation as very detrimental to the timber. One reaſon given for lopping the elm is, that it may be the better converted into a hollow trunk to convey water under ground. Elm is the wood chiefly uſed for this purpoſe, as it continues long ſound if it be kept from the air; but perhaps not one in fifty of theſe mutilated trees is converted to this uſe.

Guildford is a town both of antiquity and curioſity; but is in no part picturesque. It conſiſts of one long ſtreet, running down precipitately to the river Wey; from whence the road on the other ſide riſes ſtill more abruptly.

ruptly *. In the higheft part of the town
ftands the caftle, which confifts of a heavy
tower, though in one or two points it is not
unpicturefque. The Wey is navigable as far
as Guildford; and beyond it, for timber, which
is brought down the river from the contiguous
parts of the country.

Floats of timber are among the pleafing appendages of a river, when the trunks are happily difpofed. This difpofition, however, I
fear, muft be the refult of chance, rather than
of art. It is hardly poffible to pack a float picturefquely by defign. Thefe cumbrous machines are navigated each by a fingle man with
a pole; and as they glide gently down the
ftream, the tremulous reflections they form on
the ftill furface of the water, and their contraft
with trees, bufhes, and pafturage, as they float
along, are pleafing.

But cumbrous as thefe rafts are, they are as
nothing compared with thofe which are often
floated down the Rhine. In the neighbourhood
of Andernach, great quantities of timber,
brought down by various ftreams, from the
forefts of Germany, are there conftructed into

* It has lately been much eafed.

a float

a float of vaft dimenfions. Some of thefe floats
are a thoufand feet long, and ninety broad;
and are each furnifhed with five hundred men.
For the accommodation of fuch a company, a
ftreet of cabins is built upon the furface of the
float. When all is ready, and the feveral men
are at their pofts, (many of whom are in rafts
and boats, both behind and before the float, to
conduct it properly,) the pilot ftands up, and
taking off his hat, with a loud voice cries out,
" Let us pray:" on which the whole body of
the workmen on board fall down on their
knees, and beg a bleffing on the expedition.
The anchors and cables are then drawn on board,
and the whole machine is put in motion. As it
fails majeftically down the Rhine, it draws all
the inhabitants from the towns and villages on
the banks of the river to fee it pafs, till it arrive at Dort in Holland, the place of its defti-
nation; where being broken up, the fale of its
feveral parts continues many months, and
raifes often the fum of thirty thoufand pounds*.

To thefe timber floats we may add one of a
very fingular kind on the Nile, conftructed of
earthen veffels. Large jars, to preferve water

---

* See a longer account of thefe floats in a very ingenious
and entertaining work, intitled " A Journey through Holland,
" &c. by Anne Ratcliffe."

in

in dry feafons, are in great requeft in many parts of Egypt. Thefe, of various fizes, are manufactured chiefly in the clayey grounds of the upper parts of the country. When the potter has gotten a fufficient number ready for market, he begins to form his float. In fome convenient place near the river, he ranges his largeft jars, empty, but well-corked, in rows of a proper length and breadth. Thefe he braces tight with flexible twigs: and with the fame art ranges above them feveral tiers of fmaller jars, till he has made up the quantity and kind of goods his market demands. Over all he conftructs a feat for himfelf. By this time the waters of the Nile, whofe increafe he calculates, begin to ripple round his earthen raft, which is prefently after afloat. Having victualled it with a bag of parched rice, and put on his blue linen fhirt and cap, he takes his feat, and paddles his veffel into the middle of the channel. The wondering ftranger eyes from the fhore this odd fpecies of navigation; and though affifted by his pocket-perfpective, cannot conceive its conftruction. In the mean time it glides down the ftream. Neither ftorms nor rocks it fears, with which the Nile is little acquainted; and if

it

it even touch the ground, its motion is so gentle, and the ooze so soft, that its construction is not in the least disturbed. Nothing can be more ingenious than to make a cargo of heavy materials its own vehicle; at the same time, such a float could hardly be an object of beauty.

The elegant author of the *Elegy in a Churchyard* seems to have had a float of this kind in his view, in the last lines of the following beautiful description of the Nile.

> What wonder, in the sultry climes that spread,
> Where Nile (redundant o'er his summer-bed)
> From his broad bosom, life and verdure flings,
> And broods o'er Egypt with his watry wings,
> If with adventurous oar, and ready sail,
> The dusky people drive before the gale;
> Or, on *frail floats* to neighbouring cities ride,
> That rise, and *glitter* o'er the ambient tide.

From Guildford to Farnham the form of the country is singular. The road is carried through the space of eight miles, over a ridge of high ground with a steep descent on each side. This grand natural terrace, which the country people call the *Hog's back*, presents on each hand extensive distances. On the

right

right the diftance is very remote, confifting of that flat country through which the Wey, the Mole, and the Thames, though none of them objects in the fcene, flow with almoft imperceptible motion. On the left the diftance is more broken with rifing grounds interfperfed through various parts of it.

Though the diftance on neither hand forms a picture, except in a few places, for want of foregrounds and proper appendages proportioned to the fcene; yet on both fides we ftudy a variety of thofe pleafing circumftances, which we look for in remote landfcape. As we draw near the clofe of this terrace, the two diftances unite in one, forming a kind of grand amphitheatre in front.

Such violent contrafts as thefe, in which lofty grounds break down *precipitately* into extenfive plains, are rather uncommon in nature, as thefe different modes of country are generally more imperceptibly united. We have feveral fcenes, however, of this kind in different parts of England; particularly in the view over the vale of Mowbray * ; and in that over the vale of Severn † ; in both which the union is abrupt.

* See Northern Tour, vol. ii. p. 191.
† See the Wye, p. 8.

As

As England, however, is a country only on a small scale, compared with the vast tracts on the continent, its scenes are more in miniature. Its rivers, its lakes, its mountains, and plains, though generally more picturesque, as more suited to human vision, yet do not strike the imagination with so much grandeur. Many instances might be brought from the continent of sublimer effects in all modes of landscape. A very abrupt transition from the most magnificent sylvan scenery to entire sterility, I met with lately in an account of the productions of Boutan and Thibet, communicated in the Philosophical Transactions *. Where Boutan, says the author of those remarks, joins the territory of Thibet, the boundary is marked by such a line, as is perhaps hardly to be seen in any other part of the earth. From the eminence where we stood, the mountains of Boutan, which ranged above us, appeared every where beautifully arrayed in wood, mantling down to our very feet. This view was towards the south. When we turned towards the north, the eye is received by a vast dreary waste, descending far and wide, composed of extensive

* Vol. lxxix.

ranges

ranges of hills and plains; but, from the woody fpot where we ftood, through the whole unbounded diftance, there is not the leaft appearance of vegetation.

Farnham confifts chiefly of one long, thorough-fare ftreet, and is principally remarkable for its being the fummer-refidence of the Bifhop of Winchefter.

Farnham-caftle ftands high, and was formerly a fortrefs of confiderable reputation. It was built by a Bifhop of Winchefter in the time of King Stephen, when caftles were much in fafhion, and made fome figure in the troubled reign of that prince. It afterwards figured in the times of Lewis the Dauphin, in the infurrections of the barons, and in the civil wars of the laft century. During thefe laft troubles it was blown up by Sir William Waller; though not with that *picturefque judgment* with which many caftles in thofe times were demolifhed. Very little is left that can make a pleafing picture. After the reftoration it depofited its military character, and was changed again into an epifcopal palace by Bifhop Morley; but it has ever fince been neglected. The prefent

fent bifhop is the firft who has paid any attention, for many generations, to Farnham-caftle.
He has greatly improved the houfe, and has
fitted it up in fuch a manner, as will probably
make it an object to every future bifhop. The
keep, or inner caftle, is left ftanding in its
ruins, and is ftill a curious piece of antiquity.
It is furrounded by a deep ditch, which, together with the area of the caftle, containing
about two acres, makes an excellent kitchen-
garden.

Behind the houfe extends a park, about four
miles in circumference, which the bifhop found
as much neglected and out of order as the
houfe itfelf. It was cut with unlicenfed paths,
the trees were mangled to browze the deer,
and a cricket ground had fo long been fuffered,
that the people conceived they had now a right
to it. This laft was a great nuifance. Such
a fcene of riot and diforder, with ftands for
felling liquor, juft under the caftle windows,
could not eafily be endured. The bifhop took
the gentleft methods he could to remove the
nuifance ; and at length, though not without
fome difficulty, got it effected.

Having thus removed nuifances from his
park, he began to embellifh it. He improved

the

the furface, he laid out handfome roads and walks, he planted young trees, and protected the old trees from farther ill ufage.

Acrofs the park runs an avenue a mile long, of ancient elms. The bifhop could not per-fuade himfelf to remove this monument of an-tiquity ; and I think with great judgment hath left it in its old form ; for though an avenue is neither a pleafing nor a picturefque arrange-ment of trees, yet the grandeur of this gives it confequence ; and its connection with the an-tiquity of the caftle gives it harmony. Here the poet, after mourning the lofs of other ave-nues, may exult :

> Ye fallen avenues ! once more I mourn
> Your fate unmerited : once more rejoice
> That yet a remnant of your race furvives.

About a quarter of a mile from the houfe arifes in the park an eminence, on which ftands a keeper's lodge. The fituation is confpicuous, but the object unpleafing. A few acres, there-fore, around it are inclofed, a green-houfe is built to fkreen the lodge, and walks are cut, and adorned with different kinds of curious fhrubs in high perfection.

From this eminence are feveral openings into the country, particularly one towards

Moor-

Moor-park, where that enlightened genius, Sir William Temple, (retiring in difguft from ftate affairs, when Charles II.'s politics received a tincture from France,) cultivated every part of literature with an elegance of tafte uncommon at that day. His heart lies buried, according to his will, in a filver urn, under a dial in his garden. A fingularity of this kind, in prefer-ring a garden to a church-yard, rather favours the opinion which Bifhop Burnet gives us, of Temple's religious fentiments.

In moft of the views from the park at Farn-ham-caftle, Crookfbury-hill is a diftinguifhed feature; which, tradition fays, Sir William Temple always confidered as one of the greateft ornaments of his place. This fhews his love for nature; though in laying out his grounds, the awkward idea of the times mifled both his theory and practice.

From the terrace before the caftle, the view is fingular. We overlooked the town of Farnham, and a tract of country, which may properly be called the *vale of hops:* for we faw nothing but ranges of that plant, which was now in full leaf, and made a curious, though very unpleafing, appearance. The hop and the vine, in a *natural* ftate, are among the

I   moft

moft picturefque plants. Their fhoots, their tendrils, their leaves, their fruit, are all beautiful: but in their cultured ftate they are perfect famples of regularity, ftiffnefs, and uniformity; which are, of all ideas, the moft alien to every thing we wifh in landfcape.

Nothing fhews fo much the prejudice of names, as the value fixed on Farnham hops. Thofe produced in this parifh fell at Weyhill, and all the great fairs, at a confiderably greater price than thofe which grow even in the next parifh, though divided only by a hedge. To keep up this idea of excellence, the Farnham farmers agree every year on a fecret mark, which they affix to all their own bags. The value of the hops, fpread under our eye from the terrace on which we ftood, was fuppofed to be at leaft ten thoufand pounds.

S E C T. IV.

FROM Farnham to Alton, the road paſſes through pleaſant lanes. Holt Foreſt occupying the left, forms an agreeable woody horizon. Sometimes it breaks the line, and advances a little nearer the eye; but it generally keeps the ſame diſtance, and runs along the higher grounds, through the ſpace of ſeveral miles. But though it is higher than the neighbouring country, it is itſelf a tract of level land. We rode through it, and were much pleaſed with its woods and lawns.

In the midſt of it ſtands a houſe which formerly belonged to Mr. Bilſon Legge. A very extenſive lawn is cleared before it, interſperſed with combinations of trees; and though it is a perfect flat, yet the line of its woody boundary being varied, and removed to different diſtances by retiring woods, the whole has a good effect; which is not a little aſſiſted by ſome handſome trees on the foreground.—A flat, if it be *very extenſive*, may convey a *grand*

idea;

idea; but when we have a *small piece* of *flat* ground to improve, all we can do, unlefs we vary its furface, is to adorn it with wood. Surrounded with artful fcenery, as it is here, it may form a landfcape in which the eye may find great entertainment. The water which adorns this lodge, we thought but indifferently managed; though we were told it was contrived by the late Lord Chatham.

From Alton to Alresford, and from thence to Winchefter, we find little that excites attention. The road is in general clofe, till within a few miles of Winchefter, where the downs begin to open. They are heavy uninterefting fwells of ground: but as we proceeded farther, we admired fome of the interfections of their vaft heaving forms, and had at leaft the pleafure of furveying a large tract of country in its original ftate; on which neither Romans, Saxons, Danes, nor Britons feem to have made any impreffion *.

* More impreffion has been made on thefe downs within thefe laft half dozen years, than had been made before in as many centuries. Large portions of them are now inclofed, and thrown into tillage.

In

In a valley among thefe downs, watered by a confiderable ftream, lies Winchefter. As we defcend into it, the great church, and the *King's Houfe*, as it is called, are capital features, and give it an air of grandeur.

The fouth fide of the great church is a piece of heavy unadorned Gothic. But this was owing to accident. Formerly the buildings of a monaftery covered this fide of it, and the architect, William of Wickham, who could not forefee the diffolution of monafteries, thought it of no confequence to adorn a part of his church, which could never be feen. But when the monaftery was removed, the defect became glaring.—— Why the tower, in the hands of fo elegant an architect, was left fo ill proportioned, is a queftion of furprife. It certainly contributes to give the whole building an air of heavinefs. I doubt whether a fpire was ever intended, as it was not, I believe, among the Gothic ornaments of that day.

The infide, however, of this cathedral is very grand, except about the tranfept, where there feems to have been fome awkward contrivance. The nave, which is three hundred

feet

feet in length, is perhaps the moſt magnificent in England. But it is injured by ſome monuments, particularly that of the founder, which treſpaſs upon it: they are placed between the pillars, and bulge out into the middle aiſle of the nave. Indeed I know not whether monuments at all in ſuch churches as pride themſelves on their architecture, can in any ſhape be conſidered as ornamental: the nave of Weſtminſter-Abbey, for inſtance, is injured, *as a piece of architecture*, by the ſeveral monuments introduced into it, which, like ſpots of light in a picture, injure the *whole*; they break in upon its ſimplicity and grandeur. Thus too I doubt whether the introduction of monuments will be any advantage to St. Paul's. I ſhould fear they might injure the grandeur of the dome, which the judicious architect had already adorned, as much as he thought conſiſtent with the ſublimity of his idea. In all cathedrals there are cloiſters and other receſſes, which are the proper ſituations for monuments: and even here every thing ſhould not be admitted that comes under the name of a monument, and pays the fee. Plain tablets may be allowed; but when figures and ornaments are introduced, they ſhould be ſuch as neither diſ-

grace

grace the fculptor, nor the perfon whom he meant to honour. It would be of great advantage alfo to clafs monuments, as we hang pictures in a room, with fome view to fymmetry and order; and, if different profeffions were ranged by themfelves, it would ftill make it more agreeable to examine them.

The choir of Winchefter cathedral is greatly adorned, but without any tafte. The *love of ornament* is one of the greateft fources of deformity; and it is the more to be lamented, as it is very *expenfive*, and very *univerfal*. It prevails from the churchwarden, who paints the pillars of his parifh-church blue, and the capitals yellow; to the artift, who gilds and carves the choir of a cathedral. A tafte of this kind prevails here.

In the firft place, the fituation of the organ feems injudicious. A view along the whole range of the church, no doubt, is grand; but not, I think, of confequence to remove the organ into the awkward fituation in which it now ftands, in the middle of one of the fides, where it has no correfpondent part: befides, an organ, if judicioufly adorned, is a proper finifhing to one end of the choir, as the communionmunion-table and its appendages, are to the other.

The wood-work in the choir is elegant Gothic ; but it is greatly injured by a blue band, fpangled with golden ftars, with which the ground behind it is adorned. What the meaning of this ftrange conceit is, I could not conjecture.

But the decoration of the altar-piece is the moft offenfive. The choir is feparated from the chapels beyond it, by a lofty fcreen. The tabernacle work of this fcreen ftill remaining, fhews it to have been of the pureft Gothic. It is divided into twelve compartments, which are fuppofed to have held ftatues of the twelve apoftles. But thefe having been deftroyed in the time of the civil wars, each Gothic niche is injudicioufly filled with a Roman urn.

But the projection over the communion-table is ftill more offenfive. It is a fort of penthoufe hanging over the table, and adorned with feftoons of flowers. They are faid to have been carved by Gibbons, and probably were; but all the elegant touches of his chifel are deftroyed. At Hampton Court, at Chatfworth, and wherever we have the works of this

master,

mafter, great care has been taken to preferve them in their original purity. I believe not even a varnifh has been fuffered. But here they are daubed all over with brown paint, totally at variance with every thing around them ; and as if that were not enough, they are alfo adorned with profufe gilding.

Infhrined amidft all this abfurdity, hangs Weft's picture of the Refurrection of Lazarus, which is by no means, in my opinion, among the beft works of this mafter. The *compofition* did not pleafe me. The whole is divided formally into three parts, with too little connection among them. Jefus and his difciples ftand on one fide, the fpectators on the other ; Lazarus and his fifters occupy the middle. Neither is the *effect of light* nor the *harmony of the colouring* more pleafing. The colouring particularly, which both the ftory and the fituation of the picture required to be peculiarly modeft, is inharmonioufly glaring. The *parts* did not appear to more advantage than the *whole*. There is but little of thofe paffions, and varied expreffion, which the ftory is meant to excite. In *drawing*, Mr. Weft is acknowledged to be a perfect mafter. But there is one thing in the picture which is particularly

E   difpleaf-

difpleafing. Every painter fhould fo far provide for the *diftant effect* of his picture, that no
improper or difagreeable idea may be excited
in the *general view* of it. As you approach
this picture, without knowing what the fubject
is, a figure at the foot of Lazarus gives the
whole too much the appearance of *une femme
accouchée.*

The fkreen which feparates the choir from
the nave and the aifles, is beautiful *in itfelf*;
but we are aftonifhed that fuch an artift as
Inigo Jones fhould not fee the abfurdity of
adorning a Gothic church with a Grecian
fkreen. The ftatues of James I. and Charles I.
however they come there, would have been in
themfelves more pleafing, if their unclaffical
infignia of crowns and fceptres had been removed.

The *King's Houfe* was built by Sir Chriftopher Wren for Charles II. It ftands on the
fite of the old caftle of Winchefter, loftily
overlooking the city, and is, I think, a beautiful
piece of architecture. Magnificent it certainly
is, extending in front above three hundred
feet; and if it had been completed in the
grand ftyle in which it was conceived, with its
lofty cupola, and other appendages; its gardens

dens and parks laid out in ample fpace behind;
a noble bridge in front over the ditch ; and
the ftreet opened, as was intended, to the weft
end of the cathedral, with which its front is
parallel; it would have been perhaps one of
the grandeft palaces in Europe. The death of
Charles put an end to the fcheme. It had
afterwards another chance of being completed;
having been fettled on Prince George of Den-
mark, if he had furvived Queen Anne. Its
laft tenants were fix thoufand French prifoners,
from whofe dilapidations it will not fpeedily
recover *.

Winchefter was not only a regal feat in
Saxon times, but one of the firft towns in Britain. Its hiftory is full of curiofity ; and the
antiquities with which it abounds confirm its
hiftory : but among its antiquities I recollect
no *object of beauty*, except an old crofs in the
high ftreet, which is an exquifite piece of Gothic architecture ; and fhews that the artifts of
thofe days could *adapt their ideas of proportion*
as well to works of miniature as of grandeur.
This little ftructure rifes from a bafement of

---

* It has fince been much more refpectably occupied by a
body of emigrant French priefts ; but is now, I believe, converted into a barrack.

E 2   half

half a dozen fteps, with curious open work, in a pyramidal form. It is ornamented in the richeft manner; but its ornaments are becoming, becaufe they are introduced with proportion, uniformity, and fymmetry. If the edges had been gilt and adorned with Chinefe bells, it would have been ornamented in a tafte fomething like that employed in the choir of the cathedral.

S E C T. V.

FROM Winchefter to Salifbury the road ftill continues along downs, the parts of which often fold beautifully over each other. This fort of country, though in itfelf unpicturefque, affords a good ftudy for a landfcape-painter. It gives him a few large mafterly ftrokes, and forms an outline which the imagination fills up. About a mile fhort of Stockbridge, we had a good diftance on the left.

As we gain the higher grounds about two or three miles before we reach Salifbury, the lofty fpire of the cathedral makes its firft appearance, and fixes the fpot to which the road, though devious, will certainly carry us at laft. It is amufing to fee a deftined point before us, as we come up to it by degrees. It is amufing alfo to transfer our own motion to that of the object we approach. It feems, as the road winds, to play with us, fhewing itfelf here and there, fometimes totally difappearing, and then rifing where we did not expect to find it. But the moft pleafing circumftance in approaching

E 3   a grand

a grand object, confifts in its depofiting by degrees its various tints of obfcurity.   Tinged at
firft with the hazy hue of diftance, the fpire
before us was but little diftinguifhed from
the objects of the vale.   But as it was much
nearer than thofe objects, it foon began to affume a deeper tint, to break away from them,
and leave them behind.   As we get ftill nearer,
efpecially if a ray of funfhine happen to gild
it, the fharp touches on the pinnacles fhew the
richnefs of its workmanfhip, and it begins
gradually to affume its real form.

Salifbury is a pleafant town, with the fweet
accommodation of a ftream of limpid water
running through every ftreet.   But the only
thing in it worth the attention of a picturefque
eye, is the great church and its appendages.

Salifbury cathedral is efteemed the only pure
fpecimen we have of the early ftyle of Gothic
architecture.   It marks the period when Saxon
heavinefs began firft to give way.   It wants
thofe light and airy members which we find
in the cathedrals of York, Canterbury, Lincoln,
and others of a later period : but it poffeffes
one beauty which few of them poffefs, that
of fymmetry in all its parts.   The fpire is
efteemed the loftieft ftructure of the kind in
England.

England. It is very light: yet its great height, especially when seen either from the east or west, appears rather disproportioned; and indeed, on the whole, I think, no spire can be so pleasing an object as an elegant Gothic tower. The tower is capable of receiving all the beauties of Gothic ornament. Those of many of our cathedrals, indeed of many of our parish churches, as of Derby for instance, are adorned with great elegance; but the spire, tapering to a point, does not present a sufficient surface for ornament. The bands round that of Salisbury are rather a deformity: nor do I see what Gothic ornaments so tapering a surface is capable of receiving; for which reason, though a plain well-proportioned spire may happily adorn a neat parish church, and make a picturesque object rising among woods, or in the horizon, I think it is not so well adapted to the rich style of a Gothic cathedral: and indeed succeeding architects, as the Gothic taste advanced in purity, laid aside the spire, and in general adopted the tower. Pinnacles, which are purely Gothic, are very beautiful: and for this reason the tower part, or foundation of the spire at Salisbury, which is adorned with them, is the only part of it that is interesting.

If

If inftead of the fpire, fomething of a Gothic
dome, or rich open work, had been carried up
a moderate height, I think it would have been
more beautiful. As it is, the chief idea feems
to have been to carry ftones higher into the
air, than they were ever carried before.

The infide of Salifbury cathedral is more
beautiful than the outfide. The affemblage of
its various parts, fo harmonious among themfelves, and its fimple ornaments, though of
the rudeft Gothic, are very pleafing.

There is one beautiful circumftance in it
which I remember not to have feen, with fo
good an effect. in any other cathedral, except
that of Wells. To the eaft end of the choir
St. Mary's chapel is attached; and appears feparated from it only by three large pointed
open arches behind the communion-table.
The internal part of the chapel, with its eaft
window and pillars, feen through thefe arches,
gives the conjunct idea of fpace and perfpective, which is very pleafing.

But this cathedral alfo, though in itfelf a
noble piece of architecture, has been much injured by what is called *beautifying*. The nave
of the church and fide aifles were painted, as if
they had been arched with brick. Nothing
could

could be more abſurd or diſguſting. The choir
alſo was coloured with three tints; which had
a bad effect. If the whole had been waſhed
with one uniform ſtone-colour, the natural
lights and ſhades would have been ſeen to
more advantage. The prebendal ſtalls alſo,
and the organ, were all decorated in the ſame
awkward manner. The ceiling too was patched
over with circles containing ugly figures of le-
gendary ſaints: and indeed the whole was a
profuſion of bad taſte.

To remove all this deformity, and beautify
the cathedral, Mr. Wyatt was engaged by the
Biſhop and Chapter, and fully anſwered the
expectation that was raiſed. The figures on
the roof are obliterated. The whole is waſhed
over with one uniform ſtone-colour; and the
ornaments of the Biſhop's ſeat and the prebendal ſtalls are beautiful; though rather perhaps
in a ſtyle of later Gothic than the reſt of the
church.

Acroſs the middle of the choir, from wall to
wall, juſt under the roof, ran a maſſy beam
eighty feet long, and four feet ſquare. It was
a very diſguſting incumbrance; but as it had
reſted there beyond the memory of man, and
was thought to bind the two walls together, to
prevent

prevent their fpreading, it had never been touched. Mr. Wyatt, however, examined it, and being perfuaded it had no connection with the walls, ventured to remove it ; and has done it without any bad confequence. It was fup-ported in two or three places by fcaffolding ; and the middle part being fawn and taken away, the ends were eafily removed.

The next queftion was, what fhould be done with the three large arches which open the view into St. Mary's chapel ? Should they be filled with tracery-work, like the eaft win-dows of fome cathedrals ? Or, fhould they be left open, as they had always been ? The latter mode, which was certainly the better, was adopted. Tracery-work would have been out of place in this cathedral ; which was built be-fore that mode of ornament was introduced. Befides, a great beauty would have been loft, which arifes from a perfpective view into the chapel.

This queftion being fettled, another arofe. A very beautiful altar-fkreen was conftructed out of the ornaments of a little chapel, which had formerly been attached to the church, and which Mr. Wyatt found it neceffary to re-move. The queftion was, where fhould this

fkreen

ſkreen be placed? Some thought it might be
placed beſt at the end of St. Mary's chapel, ſo
that it might be ſeen to advantage through the
arches, which were to be left open entirely to
the bottom. In this caſe the communion-table
was to be moveable; and to be brought forward into the choir only when it was wanted.
Others were of opinion, that the communion-
table ſhould ſtand fixed where it had ever
ſtood; and the ſkreen, which was a very low
one, ſhould be placed juſt behind it, ſo as
merely to hide the *baſes* of the pillars, and the
pavement of St. Mary's chapel; permitting at
the ſame time a perſpective view into it above
the ſkreen. The former of theſe opinions pre-
vailed, though ſome thought it might have been
more *proper*, and more in *taſte*, to have taken
the latter. It might have been more *proper*,
becauſe it would have made a ſeparation between the church and the chapel, which is as
deſirable at one end, as the ſeparation made by
the ſkreen and the organ, between the choir
and nave, is at the other. Beſides, the communion-table is a natural adjunct to the choir,
and could not be removed, without making an
improper break. It might alſo be thought in-
decent by many people, and give offence. This
ſeparation

feparation might likewife have been more in *tafte*, becaufe the eye, not having fo good a criterion of diftance as would be afforded by feeing the *bafes* of the pillars, and *pavement* of the chapel, would have conceived the diftance to the eaft-window of the chapel greater than it really is : fo that the idea being thus in part curtailed, would in fact have been enlarged. It is an undoubted rule in painting, that an *exact delineation* of a grand object injures its fublimity. Whatever is difcretely left to the imagination is always improved. Thefe remarks, however, are founded only in theory ; and it is poffible the fkreen may have a better effect where it ftands at prefent.

The eaft window of St. Mary's chapel is adorned with a picture of the Refurrection, in painted glafs. Sir Jofhua Reynolds gave the defign ; in which, though he had reprefented our Saviour rifing, he had left the tomb ftill clofed and fealed. The Bifhop remonftrated, that he had given the fact contrary to the truth of Scripture ; where, it is faid, the feal was broken, and the ftone removed. Sir Jofhua, however, ftill perfifted ; contending, that by not breaking the feal, he had made the miracle fo much the greater ; and it was not without

7   fome

fome difficulty that the Bifhop got him perfuaded to correct his defign.   The truth, I
fuppofe, was, Sir Jofhua had not fully, at firft,
attended to the circumftances of the ftory; and
did not care to be at the trouble of altering his
picture.   How far this window, in the hands
of fo eminent a mafter, may be beautiful, I
know not.   It was not finifhed when I was
laft at Salifbury.   But if it be not better than
the other eaft-window, given by Lord Radnor,
(which is efteemed good in its kind,) it will in
my judgment be a difagreeable ornament.   Indeed, if colours cannot be better blended on
glafs, and harmonized, than I ever faw them,
I own I fhould never wifh to fee an hiftorical
fubject painted in this way.   The gloom of a
painted window in an old cathedral is pleafing: but I fhould defire only ornamental
fcrawls.   The beft painted windows I remember to have feen, were (I believe, in the chapel) at Magdalen College in Oxford.   They
are fingle figures, and only in clair obfcure.
They are the beft, becaufe they are the leaft
glaring.

The choir of Salifbury cathedral, thus improved under the able hands of Mr. Wyatt, is
now one of the moft beautiful pieces of Gothic
archi-

architecture in England. The deformities of the nave and grand aisles, I fear, will not soon be removed; as there is a deficiency in the fund ; but they greatly call for improvement.

Adjoining to the church is a square cloister opening into a chapter-house. In abbies, we suppose, the cloister was a place for the monks to enjoy exercise under cover. But, from the connection of this cloister with the chapter-house, we are led to imagine it was intended also as a place for tenants and suitors to wait under shelter, till each was called into the chapter-house to settle his respective business. The chapter-house and cloisters are in the same way connected at Gloucester ; and may probably be so in other cathedrals.

The cloister and the chapter-house at Salisbury belong to an age of much better taste in architecture than that of the cathedral itself. They are both of very pure and elegant Gothic. The former is a light airy square of about forty feet on each side. The latter is an octagon of fifty feet in diameter, with a pointed roof, supported by a light column (rather perhaps too light) in the centre. Nothing in architecture, I think, can be more pleasing than these buildings ; nor does any thing militate

so

fo much againſt a fervile attachment to the five
orders. The Greek and Roman architecture,
no doubt, poffefs great beauty : but why ſhould
we fuppofe them to poffefs *all* beauty? If men
were left to their own genius and invention,
(as the founders of the Gothic probably were,)
we might, it is true, have many abfurd compofitions, which we have even *now*; but we
ſhould certainly have greater *variety*; and
amidſt that variety, no doubt, feveral new and
elegant models. But the five orders have
drawn the art fo much to themfelves, that it
would be herefy in architecture to oppofe their
canons.

Rules, we allow, muſt confine *every art*;
but what rules are neceffary to confine *architecture*, except thofe of *utility, ſymmetry, proportion*, and *ſimplicity ?* *Utility* refpects the purpofes for which an edifice is raifed ; *ſymmetry*
the general purity and famenefs of the ſtyle;
proportion the relation of parts; *ſimplicity* the
modeſty and propriety of ornaments. I know
not in which of thefe requifites the Gothic
does not equal the Roman. If in any it may
be thought to fail, it is in the ornamental
part.

In

In what taſte the private buildings of thoſe times were conſtructed, when Gothic architecture was in its ſplendor, we know not. It is probable they were not deſigned by the eminent profeſſors of the art, but by low mechanics, according to every man's humour, without rule or knowledge. Many of them, no doubt, were inconvenient enough, as well as wretchedly adorned. But in the *public* buildings of thoſe times, there is generally ſuch propriety of ornament; that is, each ornamental member *ariſes ſo naturally from the building itſelf*, and is ſo much of a *piece with it*, (which ſeems to be all we wiſh in ornament,) that in the beſt ſpecimens of Gothic architecture, the eye is no where offended, or called aſide by the contention of parts; but examines all, *whole* and *parts* together, in one *general view*. In the *interior*, perhaps, the Gothic architect is commonly more chaſte than in the *exterior*, in which he allows himſelf more to wanton; and indeed ſeems to have had a worſe choice of proper ornaments. But in our beſt compoſitions, the outſide as well as the inſide is highly beautiful. For myſelf, I freely own, I am as much ſtruck with the cathedral of York,

or

or with this cloifter and chapter-houfe, covered
as they are with ornaments, as with the noble
fimplicity of the cathedral of St. Paul's. Each
ftyle is beautiful.

But in comparing the Gothic and Grecian
ornaments in architecture, the comparifon holds
merely with regard to fuch ornaments as are
fanciful and ideal. In portraying or combining fuch ornaments as have *nature for their original*, either in human or in animal life, the
Gothic fculptor is in general miferably deficient. He had little knowledge of Nature in
forming, and lefs of Art in *combining :* and yet
he is often offending with fome grofs reprefentation of this kind.

In the chapter-houfe at Salifbury, for inftance, which gave occafion to thefe remarks,
amidft all that beautiful profufion of *fancied
ornaments*, fo elegant in themfelves, and fo well
adapted to the building to which they are applied, there is likewife a great profufion of
hiftorical fculpture. The feveral fides of the
room are divided into ftalls for the members of
the church. I believe there are not fewer than
fifty ; and the little angular divifions between
the ftalls are adorned with bas-relief. As Gothic workmanfhip, it is not bad ; though it is

F   very

very inferior to Roman or modern fculpture.
There is no idea either of grace or tafte, or
even of proportion in the figures themfelves;
nor in the mode of combining them. They
all reprefent fcripture ftories; fome of which
are very ill-managed. In the ftory of Noah,
two beafts are looking out of a window in the
ark, fufficient to load it; and Noah himfelf
praying at the poop is fufficient to fink it.
After the civil wars, the parliament commiffioners fat in this chapter-houfe; and have left
behind them marks of their rough ideas of religion. At this fculpture they feem to have
taken particular offence, and have hacked it
miferably. They began as they entered, on
the left; and for a while erafed every thing
before them: but they feem to have grown tired
as they proceeded in their work: the middle part,
therefore, is but little injured, and the figures
on the right are perfect. If, however, the infide of this elegant building were wafhed over
with one uniform ftone-colour, the fculpture
obtrudes itfelf fo little on the eye, that bad as it
is, it might eafily pafs unobferved. Both the
cloifter and chapter houfe are in fo decaying a
ftate, that it would require a great fum to reftore them; though there is now in the library

an

an eftimate given in about an hundred years ago, from which it appears that the whole might then have been completely repaired for 150 l. It appears alfo from another paper in the library, of ancient date, that the cathedral coft 42,000 marks in building, about twenty eight thoufand pounds; which is a much larger fum than we fhould have fuppofed it could have coft at that early day.

Near the cathedral ftands the bifhop's palace, which till very lately was one of the moft gloomy manfions that can well be imagined. It was a large incumbered houfe, with about a dozen acres of flat ground, by way of garden, lying behind it. This garden was bifected with a broad canal, and confined within an embattled wall. Such an affemblage of awkward circumftances are not often united.

The prefent Bifhop of Salifbury * has, at great expence, entirely new-modelled this gloomy palace. He has altered the rooms, enlarged the windows, made a new entrance, and given a new appearance to the whole place. One great and very expenfive improvement was, to arch over a wide drain, which

* Bifhop Barrington.

F 2   was

was carried along the whole back-front of the palace. It was paffed, at different places, by two or three bridges; and was fuch a nuifance, that we are furprifed it had been fuffered fo long.

As to the flat grounds which were bifected with the canal, laid out in viftas, and circum-fcribed by an embattled wall, it was impoffible to do more, than to remove a few of the for-malities of the place, and carry a neat gravel walk round it, which near the houfe plays among a few irregular plantations.

But one improvement he has introduced, which adds a grandeur to the garden, beyond what any epifcopal feat in England can boaft. He has brought the cathedral into it, in one of its moft pleafing points of perfpective. Be-tween the palace and the cathedral ran for-merly a wall, which included a piece of ground belonging to the bifhops of Salifbury, and ufed as a kitchen-garden.

This wall, and the kitchen-garden, Bifhop Barrington has removed; and has not only obtained a *noble object*, but he has exchanged the difagreeable appearance of a long ftraight wall, for a very grand boundary to his garden. The cloifter and chapter-houfe are the parts

7   imme-

immediately introduced, whofe feveral abutments and projections are pleafing circumftances. From thefe rifes the body of the
cathedral; and the fpire having here a larger
bafe, appears more in proportion.

About a mile from Salifbury Old Sarum formerly ftood. Its fituation and eftablifhment
were both very fingular.

Imagine the *ridge* of a hill falling into a
plain; from the end of which a part having
been artificially feparated, forms a round
knoll of about two thoufand feet in diameter.
Cooped within this narrow compafs, ftood on
a ftill higher knoll in the centre a formidable
caftle; and juft below it a cathedral. Here
alfo ftood the bifhop's palace, together with
the houfes of his chapter; and the whole was
furrounded with immenfe ditches and ramparts, which ftrike us with aftonifhment even
at this day.——So clofe a union between a
caftle and a cathedral, infulated as they were,
and feated fo loftily, muft have made a very
fingular appearance, though probably they
never had much picturefque beauty.

Many

Many retainers no doubt there were on fo large a foundation; but it does not appear that any houfes, except thofe of the chapter, were admitted within the precincts of the fortrefs. Other appendages feem to have been placed as a fuburb under its walls.

Here the bifhops of Salifbury lived like temporal princes; till king Stephen, fufpecting the bifhop of that day was attached to the emprefs Maud, difpoffeffed him of his caftle of Sarum, together with two other caftles which he held; one at Sherborn, from whence the fee had been removed by William I. and the other at the Devizes.——The caftle of Sarum was given to a Norman earl, who held a garrifon in it for the king.

This became matter of continual conteft. The clergy and the garrifon were at conftant variance. Once the bifhop and his clergy returning from a proceffion, found the gates fhut againft them.

Wearied at length by repeated infults they complained to the pope, and at length got a difpenfation to remove the fee of Salifbury to its prefent fituation. This was foon found to be fo very convenient in comparifon of the old one, that it drew the inhabitants of

Old

Old Sarum by degrees after it. The caſtle was left by itſelf; and in a few years it alſo was deſerted, and Old Sarum became only a heap of ruins. But theſe ruins, deſerted as they are, preſerve a ſubſtantial proof of their antient dignity in being repreſented by two members in parliament.

SECT. VI.

FROM Salifbury our firft excurfion was to Longford Caftle, the feat of the earl of Radnor. It was built about the time of James the Firft on a Danifh model; probably by fome architect who came into England with the queen. Its form is triangular, with a round tower at each corner; which gives it a fingular appearance. It ftands in a vale, which approaches nearly to a flat; as the Avon, which paffes through the garden, does to ftagnation. Longford Caftle therefore borrows little from its fituation. All its beauty is the refult of art, which cannot rife beyond what may be called *pleafing*. But the principal objects here are the pictures. The whole collection is good. The following we thought fome of the beft.

A Return from the Chace, by Teniers. The compofition of this mafter is rarely fo good as it is here. His colouring is always pleafing.

A boy, by Rubens.

Peter

Peter de Jode's family, by Vandyck. The heads in this picture are perfect copies from Nature.

A view of Tivoli.

A landscape by Hobima. The composition, the light, and the execution in this picture are all good.

Tobias, by Spagniolet.

Two pictures by Poussin. In these, as in many of this master's works, there is a great deficiency in point of general effect; but the classical spirit in which they are painted, with the pure taste of design and correctness in the parts, will always give value to the works of Poussin. These I think are executed with a firmer pencil and more spirited touch than most of his works.

A landscape by Ruysdaal.

Two small paintings by Callot. It is surprising with what smart touches this master enlivens his figures. His pictures have all the spirit and precision of his etchings.

But the two most admired pictures in this collection, are two landscapes by Claude, which exhibit the *rise* and *decline* of the Roman empire in a pleasing allegory. The for-

mer

mer is reprefented by a fun-rife, and the landing of Eneas in Italy : the latter by a fun-fet,
and feveral Roman buildings in ruin. Nothing can exceed the colouring of both thefe
pictures. The hazy light of a rifing fun, and
the glowing radiance of a fetting one, are
exactly copied from nature; and therefore
nicely diftinguifhed. An eye accurate in the
effects of nature, will eafily difcern with which
fpecies of light the fummit of the wave, or the
edge of the battlement is tipped. And yet
Claude has in none of his pictures that I have
feen, difcriminated the *fhadows* of the morning, which are certainly much darker than
thofe of the evening. He does not indeed
appear to have marked the difference between
them. Nor do we obferve that painters in
general are more accurate. Now and then,
with Nature before him, Claude poffibly may
give a morning-fhadow its character; but
when an effect is very rare, it appears to be
the refult of *imitation,* rather than of *principle.*

With regard to *aërial landfcape,* Claude
excelled all mafters. We are at a lofs, whether to admire more the *fimplicity,* or the *effect* of his diftances.

But

But when we have beftowed this commendation on him, we have fummed up his merit.
It all lay in colouring. We rarely find an
inftance of good compofition in any of his
pictures, and ftill more rarely an exhibition
of any grand fcene or appearance of Nature.
As he lived in Italy, he had frequent opportunities of feeing much fublime fcenery: but
as it feldom ftruck him, we cannot help in-
ferring that his genius was not fublime. If a
Dutch mafter who has feen nothing but a flat
country, introduces neither rocks, nor caf-
cades, nor the floping fides of hills, into his
pictures, it is no wonder; but if a painter
who has ftudied among the Alps and Appen-
nines rejects them, it is evident that he has no
tafte for this fpecies of fcenery. Claude and
Salvator received, or might have received,
their ideas from the fame archetypes: they
were both Italian painters: but Claude ftudied
in the Campagna of Rome; Salvator among
the mountains of Calabria. While the one
therefore admired the tamer beauties of Nature, the other caught fire and rofe to the
fublime. I do not mean to infinuate that
Claude painted like a Dutchman: but only
that his genius was lefs fublime than Salvator's.

tor's. It is true, the objects he painted are of
the *grand species :* he saw no other. But as
he seldom made the best use of them by bringing them forward, and producing *grand effects;*
it is plain he saw them with indifference ; and
we conclude it was much the same to him,
whether he painted by the side of a stagnant
canal at Harlem, or under the fall of a cascade
at Tivoli. In short, he seems to have had a
knack of colouring certain objects, skies, and
distances in particular ; and this is accounted
for by his residing chiefly in the Campagna.
——As to his figures and foregrounds, if they
do not disgust the eye, it is all we expect.
His buildings too are often unpleasing and incumbered ; and seem calculated rather to shew
his skill in architecture than in the production
of picturesque beauty.——It is saying however much in favour of Claude, that he had
been bred a pastry-cook ; and that if he did
not do all that might have been done, he did
much more than could have been expected.

SECT. VII.

OUR next expedition from Salifbury was to Stonehenge and Wilton.

Stonehenge, at a diftance, appeared only a diminutive object. Standing on fo vaft an area as Salifbury Plain, it was loft in the immenfity around it. As we approached, it gained more refpect : and we could now trace a large ditch round the whole, confined within a gentle mound. But when we arrived on the fpot, it appeared aftonifhing beyond conception. A train of wondering ideas immediately crowded into the mind. Who brought thefe huge maffes of rock together? Whence were they brought? For what purpofe? By what machines were they drawn? Or by what mechanic powers erected?

Many have attempted to folve fuch queftions as thefe, but none have gone farther than conjecture. Even the very purpofe for which thefe ftones were brought together, is not fufficiently afcertained. Mr. Walpole remarks, that whoever has examined this monument,

has

has afcribed it to that clafs of antiquity of which he himfelf was moft fond. This was at leaft the cafe of the celebrated Inigo Jones. On his return from Italy, having nothing but Italian architecture in his head, he found out that Stonehenge was a Roman ruin.

Many idle things, no doubt, have been written on this fubject. It is a happy field for conjecture. On the whole, perhaps, the laborious inquiries of Dr. Stukeley have been attended with the moft fuccefs; for though neither he nor any man could anfwer all the inquiries which curiofity is apt to make on this fubject; yet he feems to have contributed more towards a juft idea of this wonderful monument, than any other antiquarian. He has gone upon principle. He has traced it by its *meafures*, and other data, into Druid times; and (as far as appears) conviction follows his refearches. In his long difcuffion, he may, in fome parts, be whimfical; and in many certainly tedious : but allowances fhould be made for a man full of his fubject, who, of courfe, will fee many things which he fuppofes to be of confequence, and which he cannot, in few words, make apparent to others.

Of

Of thefe ftones there are an hundred and forty: and by calculation it appears, that each of the largeft of them would require the ftrength of an hundred and fifty oxen to move it.

The outer circle has been formed by a combination of two uprights and an impoft; yet each combination of thefe three ftones is detached, and without any connection with the reft, except that of coinciding in the form of a circle. Many of thefe uprights ftill remain; but only five with the impofts annexed.

The inner circle never had any impofts, but confifted only of upright ftones. Ten of thefe are ftill ftanding out of forty, of which the original number is fuppofed to have confifted.

Befides thefe circles, there are fome internal parts formed of ftones, placed eliptically; fome of which alfo have had impofts. Thefe Dr. Stukeley conceives to have been the receffes of the priefts. In this part of the circle alfo is placed a ftone, which he fuppofes to have been an altar.

Rough as all this work appears now to be, after having been expofed to the ftorms of two thoufand winters, it has been originally conftructed wlth wonderful art. All the ftones
feem

feem to have been chifeled, on the infide efpecially, with great care; and the imposts have
all been let into the uprights by mortices, and
tenons very curiously wrought.

But it is not the *elegance of the work*, but
the *grandeur of the idea*, that strikes us. The
walk between the two circles, which is a circumference of three hundred feet, is awfully
magnificent : at leaft it would have been fo, if
the monument had been entire. To be immured, as it were, by fuch hideous walls of
rock ; and to fee the landfcape and the fky
through fuch ftrange apertures muft have
thrown the imagination into a wonderful fer-
ment. The Druid, though favage in his nature, had the fublimeft ideas of the object of
his worfhip, whatever it was. He always worfhipped under the canopy of the fky, and could
not bear the idea of a roof between him and
heaven. I have known the idea fometimes
taken up by pious chriftians, who have confeffed they found their minds moft expanded,
when they worfhipped in the open air.

Stonehenge is fuppofed to be the grandeft
ftructure of the kind that exifts. We meet
with many other Druidical remains of this
form, though of inferior fize. But I have
fome-

fomewhere heard of one in France, inferior indeed to Stonehenge in magnificence, but fuperior to it in elegant conftruction. The impofts *uniting with each other*, form one continued circle of ftone on the top of the uprights; which makes a more pleafing appearance than Stonehenge, where each impoft, refting on two uprights, ftands detached from its neighbour.

Wonderful, however, as Stonehenge is, and plainly difcovering that the mind, which conceived it, was familiar with great ideas, it is totally void, though in a ruinous ftate, of every idea of picturefque beauty; and I fhould fuppofe was ftill more fo in its perfect one. We walked round it, examined it on every fide, and endeavoured to take a perfpective view of it, but in vain; the ftones are fo uncouthly placed, that we found it was impoffible to form them, from any ftand, into a pleafing fhape.

Befides thefe ftones, there are others of immenfe fize in different parts of the ifland; though none, I believe, fo large. Near Borough-bridge two or three of the largeft are found, which are known by the name of the *Devil's Arrows*.

Volney, in his Travels through Syria, mentions three ftones of white granite, among the

G   ruins

ruins of Balbeck, each of which was twelve feet thick; and which together extended above fifty-eight yards. And in an adjacent quarry, he found a ftone lying, half chifeled, which was fixty-nine feet long, and in breadth and thicknefs about thirteen. It was probably too large to be carried from the fpot *.

About two miles from Dol in Bretagne, in the middle of an orchard, Mr. Wraxall tells us, there is a fingle ftone fixed in the earth, of a conic form, which is about forty-five feet high, and nearly as many broad. It had long puzzled the antiquarians of the country, and gave rife to various conjectures. Some of them however endeavoured to get at its foundation. There they found it was really a natural production, being fixed to a ftratum of folid rock feveral feet below the furface †.

The plain, on which Stonehenge ftands, is in the fame ftyle of greatnefs as the temple that adorns it. It extends many miles in all directions, in fome not lefs than fifty. An eye unverfed in thefe objects is filled with aftonifh-

* Vol. ii. p. 241.
† Tour through France, p. 36.

ment

ment in viewing wafte after wafte rifing out
of each new horizon.

> —————— Such appears the fpacious plain
> Of Sarum, fpread like Ocean's boundlefs round,
> Where folitary Stonehenge, grey with mofs,
> Ruin of ages, nods.——

The ground is fpread, indeed, as the poet obferves, *like the ocean*; but it is like the ocean
after a ftorm, it is continually heaving in large
fwells. Through all this vaft diftrict, fcarce a
cottage or even a bufh appears. If you approach within two or three miles of the edge
of the plain, you fee, like the mariner within
foundings, land at a diftance, houfes, trees, and
villages ; but all around is wafte.

Regions, like this, which have come down
to us rude and untouched, from the beginning
of time, fill the mind with grand conceptions,
far beyond the efforts of art and cultivation.
Impreffed by fuch views of nature, our anceftors worfhiped the God of nature in thefe
boundlefs fcenes, which gave them the higheft
conceptions of eternity. Such were the grand
ideas of the patriarch, as he ranged the wide
regions of the eaft, and fet up his monumental
pile, not adorned with vafes or ftatues, but a
mound of earth, a rude pillar, which he called

G 2 *God's*

God's House, or fome vaft heap of ftones, of a fabric, firm as the ground on which it ftood, like this before us, which has feen in fucceffion the ruins of innumerable works of art, and will probably remain undiminifhed till the end of time.

All the plain, at leaft that part of it near Stonehenge, is one vaft cemetary. Every where, as we paffed, we faw tumuli or *barrows*, as they are called, rifing on each hand. Thefe little mounds of earth are more curioufly and elegantly fhaped than any of the kind I remember elfewhere to have feen. They commonly rife in the form of bells, and each of them hath a neat trench fafhioned round its bafe; though in their forms, and in the ornamental circles at their bafes, fome appear to be of more diftinguifhed workmanfhip. They are of various fizes, fometimes of thirty, fometimes of forty or fifty yards in diameter. From many places we counted above an hundred of them at once; fometimes as if huddled together without any defign; in other places rifing in a kind of order. By the rays of a fetting fun the diftant barrows are moft confpicuoufly feen. Every little fummit being tipped with a fplendid light, while the plain is in fhadow,

is

is at that time eafily diftinguifhed. Moft of
them are placed on the more elevated parts of
the plain ; and generally in fight of the great
temple. That they are manfions of the dead
is undoubted; many of them having been
opened, and found to cover the bones both of
men and beafts; the latter of which were probably facrificed at the funeral. We fuppofe
alfo that fome of them contained the promif-
cuous afhes of a multitude, as Virgil defcribes
them.

> ——Confufæ ingentem cædis acervum,
> " Nec numero, nec honore cremant. Tunc undique
>   " vafti
> " Certatim crebris collucent ignibus agri.
> " Tertia lux gelidam cœlo dimoverat umbram;
> " Mœrentes altum cinerem, et confufa ruebant
> " Offa focis ; tepidoque onerabant aggere terræ."

Indeed this mode of burial, as the moft honourable, feems to have been dictated by the
voice of nature. We meet with it in Homer;
we meet with it in Herodotus. The veftiges
of it are found on the vaft plains of Tartary;
and even among the favages of Guinea.

That we do not afcribe more antiquity to
thefe temples and cemetaries, than rightly belongs to them, the antiquarian hath fhewn by
many learned arguments. I fhall fubjoin an-

other

other of claffic origin ; from which it will appear probable, that the furniture of thefe vaft plains was exactly the fame in Cæfar's days, as it is now.

That chief, in the firft book of his Commentaries, defcribing the place, which was agreed on to be the fcene of conference between him and Arioviftus, tells us, it was an extenfive plain, in which was a large artificial mount. *Planities erat magna, et in ea tumulus terreus fatis grandis.* I tranflate *terreus* by the word *artificial,* becaufe it certainly implies fomething factitious. No correct writer, fpeaking of a *natural hill,* would ufe fuch an epithet. It would be a mere redundancy ; and juft as improper as if he had faid, *Planities erat magna terrea.* But in defcribing an *artificial mount,* it is certainly proper ; becaufe fuch a mount might have been conftructed of other materials befides *earth.*

That Cæfar's *tumulus* was intended alfo as a memorial for the dead, is probable from the common ufe of the word *tumulus* ; efpecially when accompanied with the epithet *terreus* ; for we know no other ufe for which thefe *tumuli terrei,* or *artificial mounts,* were conftructed, but that of being memorials of the dead ;

dead ; and for this ufe we know they cer-
taiuly were conftructed. We find Æneas likewife haranguing his troops from a tomb of this
kind :

—— " Socios in cætum littore ab omni
" Advocat Æneas, tumulique ex aggere fatur."

Having thus fettled Cæfar's *tumulus terreus*
to have been a *barrow* ; and knowing alfo from
him, that the Druids frequented Gaul, we are
led to believe, that his *planities magna*, and *Salifbury Plain*, were places of the fame kind ;
both of them moft probably Druid fcenes.
Cæfar indeed mentions but one tumulus on his
plain : but as he was defcribing only a particular fpot, not the general fcene, we may eafily
fuppofe there might be many other barrows,
and perhaps a Stonehenge alfo in the neighbourhood of it.

It is probable alfo, (as Cæfar tells us the
Druid difcipline was carried originally into
Gaul, from Britain, which was the great fource
of Druid-learning*,) that Salifbury Plain might

---

* " Difciplina hæc in Britannia reperta ; atque inde in Galliam
" tranflata effe, exiftimatur : et nunc, qui diligentius eam rem cog-
" nofcere volunt, plerumque illò, difcendi caufâ, proficifcuntur."
Lib. iv.

have

have been a scene of great antiquity many years before the time of Cæsar.

Though Salisbury Plain in Druid times was probably a very busy scene, we now find it wholly uninhabited. Here and there we meet a flock of sheep, scattered over the side of some rising ground; and a shepherd with his dog, attending them; or perhaps we may descry some solitary waggon winding round a distant hill. But the only resident inhabitant of this vast waste is the bustard. This bird, which is the largest fowl we have in England, is fond of all extensive plains, and is found on several; but these are supposed to be his principal haunt. Here he breeds, and here he spends his summer-day, feeding with his mate on juicy berries, and the large dew-worms of the heath. As winter approaches, he forms into society. Fifty or sixty have been sometimes seen together.

As the bustard leads his life in these unfrequented wilds, and studiously avoids the haunts of men, the appearance of any thing in motion, though at a considerable distance, alarms him. I know not that he is protected, like the partridge and pheasant, by any law; but his own vigilance is a better security to him than

an

an act of parliament. As he is fo noble a
prize, his flefh fo delicate, and the quantity of
it fo large, he is of courfe frequently the object of the fowler's ftratagems. But his cau-
tion is generally a protection againft them all.
The fcene he frequents, affords neither tree to
fhelter, nor hedge to fkreen, an enemy; and
he is fo tall, that when he raifes his neck to
take a perfpective view, his eye circumfcribes
a very wide horizon. All open attempts
therefore againft him are fruitlefs. The fowler's moft promifing ftratagem is to conceal
himfelf in a waggon. The weft country waggons, periodically travelling thefe regions, are
objects to which the buftard is moft accuf-
tomed; and though he retires at their approach, he retires with lefs evident figns of
alarm, than from any thing elfe. It is poffible
therefore, if the fowler lie clofe in fuch a con-
cealment, and with a long barrelled gun can
direct a good aim, he may make a lucky fhot.
Sometimes alfo he flips from the tail of a waggon a couple of fwift greyhounds. They foon
come up with the buftard, though he runs
well; and if they can contrive to reach him,
juft as he is on the point of taking wing, (an
operation which he performs with lefs expedition

dition than is requifite in fuch critical circumftances,) they may perhaps feize him.

Some encroachments have been made by the
plough, within thefe few years, upon Salifbury
Plain. But thefe inroads, though confiderable
in themfelves, bear little proportion to the vaftnefs of thefe downy grounds. The plough is
a heavy invader; and its perfeverance only can
produce a vifible effect in fo vaft a fcene.

Another reafon alfo may operate powerfully
in preferving thefe wide domains in a ftate of
nature. The foil is, in moft places, very fhal-
low, not above five or fix inches above a rock
of chalk; and as the tillage of two or three
years exhaufts it, without more expence than
the land will anfwer, it hath been thought but
ill hufbandry to deftroy a good fheep-walk,
for a bad piece of arable land.

But though Salifbury Plain is a remarkable
fcene in England, it is nothing in comparifon
of many fcenes of this kind on the face of the
globe, in which the eye is carried, if I may fo
phrafe it, *out of fight*; where an extent of land,
flat, like the ocean, melts gradually into the
horizon. Such are many parts of Poland and
Tartary. The plains of Yedefan, on the borders of Beffarabia, are among the moft extraordinary,

ordinary. Baron de Tott defcribes them on his journey to the Cham of Tartary, as fo immenfe, that he tells us, (fomewhat I think hyperbolically,) the piercing eyes of the Tartars, who rode before him, could diftinguifh the heads of the horfemen in the horizon, when the *convexity of the earth hid the reft of their bodies.* His defcription is more natural afterwards, when he fays, he faw the fun rife and fet on thefe plains, as navigators do at fea. Their fingularity confifts both in their vaftnefs and in certain regular vallies which bifect them. Thefe vallies are diftant from each other about ten or twelve leagues, and run in parallel lines acrofs the plain. They are totally void of the ufual ornaments of our vallies, variety of ground, a foaming rivulet, and woody banks: they are mere trenches, cut out by Nature, about twenty yards deep, and fometimes a quarter of a mile broad ; fo that as you traverfe the plain, the eye paffes over them like funk fences, and all appears one boundlefs wafte. Through the middle of each of thefe vallies is a muddy rivulet, and as there is no elevation of ground, it is almoft ftagnant. The courfe of thefe rivulets, fuch as it is, leads from north to fouth ; and at the end of the plain they form

fmall

fmall lakes, which communicate with the Black
Sea. In thefe vallies the Tartars of Yedefan
fix their tents, while their numerous herds of
horfes, oxen, dromedaries, and fheep graze the
plains. Thefe herds are continually wander-
ing from home in fummer, efpecially the larger
kinds; and the chief employment of the Tar-
tar is, to gallop about in queft of them. He
takes a quantity of roafted millet in a bag,
mounts his horfe, and rides till fun-fet. Then
if he find not what he fought, he clogs his
horfe, and leaves it to graze; and as he is always at home, he fups, wraps himfelf in his
cloak, and fleeps till morning, when he begins
his fearch again. Having given this general
account of the plains of Yedefan, Baron Tott
fpeaks of his firft day's journey over them.
The conclufion of it was the neareft valley, at
about ten leagues diftance. The fun was
now fetting; and after a long journey, " I ftill
" faw nothing before me," fays he, " but a vaft
" melancholy plain, when I fuddenly felt my
" carriage defcend, and looking out, I faw a
" range of tents, extending to the right and
" left. We croffed a rivulet over a bad bridge,
" and found three tents on the other fide out
" of the line, one of which was intended for me,

7   " It

" It was a kind of large hen-coop, conftructed
" in à circular form, with a fort of dome open-
" ing at the top, and was covered with a felt
" of camels hair. The paling was connected
" by flips of raw hides, and finifhed with
" great ftrength and delicacy *."

But of all the plains of which we meet with
any account, thofe of the deferts of Arabia are
the moft forbidding. Perhaps no part of the
globe, of equal circumference, is fo totally deftitute of Nature's bounty, and of every kind of
vegetable furniture:

————The whole
A wild expanfe of lifelefs fand and fky.

The Tartarean plains, juft defcribed, are bifected with ftreams and vallies, fuch as they
are, covered with herbage. But the barren-
nefs of the Arabian plain in no part inter-
mits. The tents, horfes, and camels of the
caravan, to which the traveller is attached, are
the only objects he fees. If he fhould fix one
end of an immenfe cord at thefe tents, the
other might be carried round, along the rim of
a boundlefs horizon, without fweeping over
any inequality. All this vaft circle is covered

* See Memoirs of Baron de Tott, vol. i. p. 46.

with

with grey fand, like the afhes of a furnace.
Over all hangs the canopy of heaven undiver-
fified by a fingle cloud to break the rays of a
fcorching fun ; while a breeze, if it can be
called fuch, glowing with heat, often fills the
air with clouds of overwhelming duft ; or totally deftroys its vital fpring.

> —————Breathed hot
> From all the boundlefs furnace of the fky,
> And the wide glittering wafte of burning fand,
> A fuffocating wind the pilgrim fmites
> With inftant death.   Patient of thirft and toil,
> Son of the defert, even the camel feels,
> Shot through his withered heart, the fiery blaft.

In the mean time a univerfal filence reigns over
the whole vaft fcene.   None of the chearful
founds of nature are heard ; neither of beaft,
nor of bird, nor even of humming infect.   All
is ftill as night.   With fuch a country as this,
Mofes threatens the people of Ifrael on their
difobedience. *The heaven that is over thy head
fhall be brafs, and the earth that is under thee
fhall be iron.   The Lord fhall make the rain of
thy land powder and duft.   From heaven fhall
it come down upon thee, till thou be deftroyed* *.
——There is, however, an appearance in thefe

* Deut. xxviii. 23, 24.

deferts, taken notice of by Sir John Chardin,
whith is rather picturefque. A fplendor or
vapour is fometimes formed by the repercuffion
of the rays of the fun from the fand, which
feems at a diftance a vaft lake. But as the
thirfty traveller approaches in hopes of finding
water, it retires before him, or totally difap-
pears *. Q. Curtius takes notice of the fame
effect in one of the marches of Alexander.

Thus we fee how *differently* Nature works up
the *fame modes* of fcenery; and there is great
amufement in bringing thefe feveral fcenes together, and in following her fteps through all
her fimilar, but varied operations.

* Sir J. Chardin's MSS. as quoted by Harmer.

SECT. VIII.

HAVING satisfied our curiosity on Salisbury Plain, and performed the due rites at Stonehenge by pacing its dimensions, and counting the stones, we proceeded to Wilton. The point of Salisbury spire, just emerging from the horizon, guided us across the open country; and as we got into the more cultivated part, we turned out of the Salisbury road, and fell down into Wilton, which lies in a vale on the edge of the plain. We cannot expect a very beautiful scene in the neighbourhood of such a waste. Nature's transitions are generally gradual. The true picturesque vale is rarely found in any country, but a mountainous one. Great plenty of wood and water however give an agreeable air to the vale of Wilton.

Wilton was once the capital of all this country, to which it gave its name. But Salisbury drawing Old Sarum within its vortex, drew Wilton also. At present this village is chiefly remarkable for the splendid palace of the Earls of Pembroke.

Wilton-

Wilton-houfe was formerly an Abbey; and
felt the full weight of the inquifition fet on
foot in the reign of Henry the Eighth. The
ladies of Wilton-abbey were accufed of too
great an intimacy with the monks of a neighbouring houfe. Stories of this kind were
liftened to at the time of the diffolution with
great attention; though often perhaps void of
any foundation. Both houfes however fell
together; and the demefnes of Wilton were
given to the Pembroke family, in whofe hands
they ftill continue. The earl of that day
began immediately to turn the abbey into
a manfion: but the plan was not completed
in its prefent ftate till late in the reign of
Charles I. The garden-front by Inigo Jones
is admired by all judges of architecture. The
portico boafts the hand of Hans Holbein.
There are fome things however yet wanting
to give the houfe an air of magnificence. The
entrance is particularly awkward and incumbered *.

As the morning threatened rain, we thought
it better to take a view of the garden, before
we entered the houfe: it occupies the centre

* Since this was written, it has been altered.

of

of a wide valley, adorned with a river. This
river was fashioned, by the conductors of taste
in the last age, into an immense canal. It is
now changed again into an irregular piece of
water. But though its banks are decorated
with rich garden-scenes, it still retains enough
of formality to suggest the old idea. It forms
however the grandest view in the garden.
Salisbury church comes in very happily as an
object at the bottom of it; and is of sufficient
magnitude to shew that it was not constructed
for the purpose.

Garden-scenes are never *picturesque.* They
want the bold roughness of nature. A principal beauty in our *gardens,* as Mr. Walpole
justly observes, is the smoothness of the turf:
but in a *picture,* this becomes a dead and uniform spot; incapable of light and shade, and
must be broken insipidly by children, dogs,
and other unmeaning figures; — that is, I
suppose Mr. Walpole means, by such figures
as commonly frequent garden-scenes, which
are of all others the most unpicturesque. And
yet I have been informed that Mr. B. Wilson
made a good landscape even of this scene.
He took it, however, from that end which is
nearest to Salisbury, where he got *a rougher*
foreground

foreground than he could find in the garden. In à *diſtance*, he might more eaſily diſguiſe a *garden-ſcene*.

Oppoſite to the houſe, the river Willy enters the canal. It is a river only of ſmall dimen-ſions, but over it is thrown a magnificent Pal-ladian bridge.

I have ſometimes thought the Palladian bridge may be conſidered as a ſpecies of bom-baſt in architecture. It is like expreſſing a plain *ſentiment* in a *pompous phraſe*. Merely to paſs a trifling ſtream, a plank with a ſimple rail is ſufficient; and in a *paſtoral* ſcene, it is all you require. In ſuch a ſcene as *this*, indeed, a ſimple plank would be *out of place*. You are compoſing *in heroics*. But a certain ſpecies of ſimplicity is required even here; and as in all *literary compoſitions* turgid expreſſions offend, why ſhould they not offend in *every* mode of compoſition? Here we allow a handſome bridge is neceſſary. But why *more* than a bridge? What have pillars—walls—pediments —and roofs to do with a bridge? A bridge in itſelf is one of the moſt beautiful of artificial objects: but dreſſed in this bombaſt ſtyle, it offends: it offends at leaſt the ſimplicity of a pictureſque eye. If you want a cool, airy

building

building to receive the refreſhment of a ſummer breeze, as it paſſes over the lake, erect one in ſome proper place, and if it be well diſpoſed, nobody can take offence. But let it ſtand for what it is. Do not leave people in doubt whether it is a houſe or a bridge, by *uniting* modes of architecture, which are in themſelves *diſtinct*; and giving one the ornaments that belong to another. From theſe criticiſms we except ſuch bridges as are ſituated, like the Rialto at Venice, which, connecting the parts of a large city, may be allowed to aſſume a correſpondent air of grandeur; and may with propriety even be covered with a roof. But here no ſuch accommodation is neceſſary; and what is unneceſſary is always affected.

From the Palladian bridge and banks of the river, the ground riſes beautifully, conſiſting of a hanging lawn, encompaſſed with wood, which is broken into pleaſing parts. But here, though in ſight of the Palladian bridge, we have another ornament full as much out of *place* as the other was out of *form.*

On the ſummit of the hill is erected a triumphal arch, with Marcus Aurelius mounted on horſeback on the top of it.

Now

Now if we only recollect the intention of a triumphal arch, we shall see how grotesquely such a fabric is erected here.

When a Roman general triumphed, it was the custom to raise these arches, through which the procession passed to the city; and they were sometimes constructed and adorned in a very magnificent manner, and left as memorials of the great event on which they were at first erected. All this was noble, and admirably adapted to the intended purpose. But we have here a triumphal arch set upon the top of a hill, totally unconnected with any thing near it. A triumphal arch would be perhaps too pompous a structure to form a part of the *approach* to the house; yet in that capacity it might have been *suffered*; it might have had some analogy at least to its situation. But as it now stands, however good it may be in itself, it is certainly an absurd ostentatious ornament.

The rain coming on obliged us to leave the rest of the garden unseen, and drove us into the house. It prevented also our seeing the stables, which are very grand; and what we still regretted more, a row of cedars of Libanon, which are esteemed the finest in England.

H 3   We

We faw them afterwards from the windows of the houfe, but probably to fome difadvantage, as they did not anfwer the expectations we had formed of them.

The grand collection of ftatues in Wilton-houfe entitle it very defervedly to the attention of every traveller. When we enter the great hall, we are ftruck with the profufion of them.

At the firft view of fuch a collection, it becomes matter of wonder how Italy can be fo inexhauftible a fund of ancient ftatues. Befides their peopling all the palaces of that country, there is not a cabinet in Europe which is not more or lefs inhabited by them. All come from Italy. Italy has been fupplying the curious with antiques for many centuries; and they who have money may buy antiques in Italy ftill.

The wonder will, in fome degree, fubfide, when we confider the rage for fculpture which poffeffed the ancient Romans. Statues were the chief ornaments of old Rome, and had for ages been collected there by all ranks of people.

The conqueft of Greece brought them firft into repute. As they became more admired; prætors and proconfuls made them every where

the

the objects of rapine. Not only Greece, but
the Ægean ifles, Afia, and Egypt, were pillaged.
Statues, bafs-reliefs, bufts, pillars, every thing
that could be fevered from the buildings to
which they belonged, were fwept away to
Rome. Temples, baths, porticoes, and other
public places, were firft adorned. The con-
quered provinces could not fupply the demand.
Artifts were called from Greece: Parian marble was imported; and ftatues were erected
to the Gods, and heroes of Rome, as had been
erected before to thofe of Greece:

——— ——— Italufque, paterque Sabinus
Vitifator, curvam fervans fub imagine falcem ;
Saturnufque fenex ; Janique bifrontis imago,
Veftibulo adftabant; aliique ab origine reges,
Martia qui ob patriam pugnando vulnera paffi.

The rage for thefe beautiful ornaments next
feized *private perfons*. Every one who had a
confular, or a prætorian anceftor, wifhed to fee
him erected in brafs or marble, till at length it
became as common in Rome to have a likenefs taken by a ftatuary, as it is in London to
have one taken by a portrait painter. Artifts,
no doubt, there were, of all kinds; and prices
adapted to every rank. The mechanic, therefore, as well as the fenator, might fee his houfe

adorned

adorned with himfelf, his wife, and his family, all fculptured to the life in ftone. Many of thefe ignoble ftatues might, in length of time, depofit their plebeian forms, and vifit foreign countries, as Scipios, Cæfars, and Octavias. It is not every connoiffeur who can detect them by their garb.

From what has been obferved, we may eafily judge what an inexhauftible fund of antiques Rome, and its colonies, (for the rage fpread over all the neighbouring parts of Italy,) might produce. Quantities, no doubt, of thefe works are ftill laid up in thofe magazines of ruin and rubbifh which Goths and other barbarous invaders have heaped upon them.

The ftatues, bufts, and bafs-reliefs, which we now furvey, were chiefly collected by the cardinals Mazarin and Richlieu; and the Earl of Arundel, in Charles the Firft's time. Additions have been made fince. Some, I have been told, were prefented by one of the Dukes of Tufcany, to whom an Earl of Pembroke had fhewn particular civilities, during his ftay in England. The collection, no doubt, is very magnificent, (one of the firft, perhaps, in Europe, if we except royal and claffic ground,) and many of its contents are excellent pieces of

art.

art. In general, however, they may be claffed,
as Martial claffes his epigrams, into good, bad,
and indifferent. It is impoffible, that in fo numerous a collection the whole can be valuable.
In many of thofe, however, which are indifferent, fome of the parts may be good, and afford
ufeful ftudies.

Among the bufts which ftruck us moft, (on
the tranfient view we were able to give them,)
were thofe of Miltiades—Hannibal—Pindar—
Adrian—Cleopatra, the fifter of Alexander—
— Lepidus — Sophocles — Pompey — Nerva—
Labienus Parthicus — Semiramis — Marcellus
the younger—Metellus imberbis—Diana—Lu-
can—Caracalla—Alcibiades—Cecrops—Vitel-
lius—and Galba. Pyrrhus of Epire is particularly fine. The air of this buft is very noble;
and is impreffed with the whole character of
the hero. A colloffean buft too of Alexander
the Great is ftriking; but the head feems rather too long. Probably it might be covered,
though I do not recollect the circumftance,
with a Grecian helmet. If fo, the head-piece
and vifor, connected without a joint, when
thrown back, would make the head too long
by the addition of the length of the face.

Among

Among the alto-relievos, we admired two
Cupids—Curtius—Saturn—fome Boys eating
grapes—Ulyffes in the cave of Calypfo—Saturn crowning the Arts—Cupid fucking Venus
—The ftory of Clælia—Silenus on his afs—
—Galatæa—Cupids and Boys—A Boy on a
fea-horfe.—A Victory, the compofition of
which is very good—A Prieftefs facrificing,
in which the animals are particularly fine—A
Nuptial Vafe, both the form and fculpture of
which are elegant.

Among the ftatues, we thought the beft
were—A fmall Meleager—An Amazonian
Queen, lefs than the life, the attitude and expreffion of which are both excellent—A dying
Hercules: part of this group is good, particularly the expreffion of Pean; but the principal
figure, though in miniature, is monftrous, and
the character is unpleafing—A Coloffean Hercules—Saturn holding a Child—The Father of
Julius Cæfar; the attitude of this figure is very
noble—Mark Anthony; the attitude of this
too is admirable—Venus holding a Vafe; this
figure, if looked at on the fide oppofite the vafe,
is pleafing, but on the other fide it is awkward.
—A Naiad, the upper part of which is beautiful—

tiful—Apollo in the Stone-hall; the body is better than the hands—Cleopatra and Cæfarion are efteemed; we did not fee much merit in them. There is at leaft no feminine beauty in Cleopatra. The pillar too in the outward court may here be mentioned; the whole of which has an elegant appearance, and the ftatue is beautiful.

It is not eafy to avoid remarking that thefe antiques might poffibly have been arranged in a more judicious manner. The *apartments* of a noble houfe fhould not fuffer their *ornaments* to obtrude *foremoft* upon the eye. Each apartment fhould preferve its *own dignity*; to which the *ornamental* part fhould be *fubordinate*. In every work of art, and indeed of nature alfo. it is a breach of the moft exprefs picturefque canon, if the *parts* engage the eye more than the *whole*. The hall, therefore, the ftaircafe, the faloon, and other apartments, might be adorned with a few bufts and ftatues; but to receive the whole collection, perhaps a long gallery fhould have been *profeffedly* built. In this they might have been arranged in *profufion*.

In conftructing fuch a gallery, little ornament would be required. Here the *ftatues*
would

would be the objects, not the *room*. To *them* therefore the *whole* fhould be fubordinate : they would conftitute the *whole*.

Two things in fuch a gallery fhould chiefly be confidered ; the colour of the walls, and the diftribution of the light. If the walls were ftained with a darkifh olive-tint, they would perhaps fhew the ftatues to the beft advantage ; and yet a lighter tinge might probably give them more foftnefs. The experiment might eafily be tried.

With regard to the *light*, it fhould be high, but not vertical. If the antiques were ranged on one fide of the room, the light might be introduced from high windows on the other. Such a light would not certainly be the moft picturefque, as each figure, at leaft when ftudied, would require a fide light, appropriated to itfelf. But this in a degree might be obtained by the means of curtains.

Much of the beauty of fuch a room would depend on the mode of arranging the antiques. The bafs-reliefs might be put in plain fquare frames, and affixed to the wall ; the bufts might ftand on brackets between them, or in receffes ; and the ftatues might occupy the front.

front. Or perhaps, on examining the whole collection together, fome more happy arrangement might be formed.

As nobody in England but the Earl of Pembroke could fit up fuch a gallery, it fhould not perhaps be made entirely a private concern. It would be generous and noble to lay it open to artifts, when well recommended; and to let them ftudy in it, under proper reftrictions. It would bring Italy, as much as could be, into England.

But ftatues are not the only furniture at Wilton: it contains many very valuable pictures.

Thofe we admired moft were,

A Cattle-piece, by Rofa of Tivoli. Few mafters are better acquainted with compofition, colouring, and the diftribution of light. This picture, though not a capital one, is an inftance of his fkill in all thefe refpects.

A whole-length of the firft Lady of the fecond Earl Philip, and a half-length of the Countefs of Caftlehaven: both thefe are by Vandyck, and both are excellent.

Mrs. Kelligrew and Mrs. Morton, by Vandyck: the latter we admired very much.

Mr.

Mr. James Herbert, by Lely.

A Carpet and Boar's-head, by Maltefe. The compofition is a ftrange one, but the picture is well painted.

An old Woman with Fifh, by Snyders. The fifh are mafterly, but the compofition is difagreeable.

An old Woman reading, by Rembrant.

Chrift taken from the Crofs, by Albert Durer. They who admire the works of the old mafters, will find a very good one here.

A large Fruit-piece, with Figures, by M. Angelo delle Battaglio. It is a tradition in the family, that M. Angelo kept this picture in his poffeffion as a favourite piece; and that Sir Robert Gere bought it of his widow for three hundred piftoles.

Democritus, by Spagnolet. The ftyle of painting in this picture is admirable; but the character of Democritus is bad.

Four Children, by Rubens. For compofition and colouring we feldom fee a more pleafing picture, either by this mafter, or any other.

The Virgin with Chrift, by Cantarini. The manner is indiftinct, but the boy is a beautiful figure.

The

The divifion of Chrift's Garments, by Carracci. This picture is well painted, but the light is ill-managed.

The Princefs Sophia, habited like a Shepherdefs, by Huntorft.

A good Virgin, by Carlo Dolce.

An admirable portrait of Titian, by himfelf.

The Woman taken in Adultery, by Janeiro. The ftory is not well told; but the figures are beautifully grouped.

A good Schalken.

An old Man felling Plumbs to Children, by Francis Hals. This is a happy fubject to fhew pleafure and difappointment in young faces; and the painter has been as happy in his expreffion of them.

In one of the rooms I remember meeting with a picture of Pietro Tefta, which is uncommon. There is great fpirit in it.

But the capital picture at Wilton, is the large family-piece by Vandyck. Of the excellence of this picture we are told many ftories; that it is Vandyck's mafter-piece; that it is celebrated through Europe; and that it might have been covered with gold, as a price to obtain it. This latter is a compliment which I have often heard paid in great houfes to favourite pictures; and

as

as the King of France is fuppofed to be the richeft man in Europe, he is generally introduced, on thefe occafions, as the bidder. For myfelf, I own I am not entirely of the King of France's opinion. I have examined this picture with great attention ; and reluctantly own I cannot bring myfelf to admire it, either in the *whole*, or in its *parts*. Vandyck's portrait of King Charles I. over a chimney at Hampton Court *, which confifts only of a fingle figure, I freely own I fhould prefer to this, though it confifts of thirteen.

Vandyck feldom appears to advantage when he has *feveral figures* to manage. His mafter Rubens early faw this, and defired him to relinquifh hiftory, and apply to portrait. He did ; but here he is again engaged in hiftory ; that is, he has a number of figures at full length to manage in one large piece, which extends twenty feet by twelve. The compofition of fuch a work required more fkill than he poffeffed.

In the firft place, there is no attempt at *defign*. Some little family-fcene fhould have been introduced, which might have drawn the figures *into one action*. Thus Titian reprefents

* I believe it is now removed.

the

the Cornaro family joining in an act of devotion *. Without fomething of this kind, the
figures had better have been painted in *feparate pictures*.

Compofition too is wanting as well as *defign*.
The figures are ill-grouped, and produce *no whole*.

The *colouring* too is glaring. Yellow, red,
and blue are the fources, when *properly blended*,
of every harmonious tint ; but here they ftare
in raw colours. Every gaudy figure ftands
foremoft to catch the eye ; except the principal figures, which are attired in black. The
young people are all fo richly dreffed, that it
feems as if their father and mother had ordered
them to put on their beft clothes, and come
down to be painted : and that the painter had
drawn them fo attired, juft as he faw them,
without any diftinction or choice of drapery.
To deftroy the harmony ftill more, a large ef-
cutcheon of the Pembroke arms hangs in one
corner of the picture, filled with fuch a profufion of red and yellow, that it catches the eye
at once, and may properly be called one of the
principal figures.

If from a *general* view of the picture, we
proceed to *particulars*, I fear our criticifms muft

* This picture belongs to the Duke of Northumberland.

I

be

be equally fevere. Never painter, it muft be owned, had that happy art which Vandyck poffeffed, of turning earths and minerals into flefh and blood. Never painter had that happy art of compofing a fingle figure with the chafte fimplicity of nature, and without affectation or artifice of any kind ; and fome of the figures in this picture are, no doubt, compofed in this ftyle, particularly the Earls of Pembroke and Carnarvon. But the figures in general, when confidered apart, are far from capital. Some of the attitudes are forced: you look in vain for Vandyck's wonted fimplicity. But what difgufts us moft, is a want of harmony. In all pictures, whether the faces are old or young, the *fame coloured light*, if I may fo exprefs myfelf, fhould be fpread over all,—the mellow or the bluifh tinge, arifing from the ftate of the atmof-phere, whatever it is, through which the light is thrown upon them : but here this rule is fo far from being obferved, that even allowing the variation of different complexions, the faces of all, though of one country, belong to different climates. A yellow-faced boy parti-cularly, among the front figures, has a com-plexion, which nothing but a jaundice or an Indian fun could have given him. For the reft,

reft, fome of the carnations are very beautiful ;
particularly the hands of the Countefs of Pembroke.

All this cenfure, however, muft not be laid
to the charge of Vandyck. His pencil could
never have been guilty of fuch violence againft
Nature. I have been affured *, that about a
dozen years ago, this picture was retouched by
a painter, I think, of the name of Brompton.
I faw it before that time, and fome years after;
and as far as my memory ferves, it was altered
much for the worfe. This may account for
moft of the faults that may be found with the
carnations.

It would have been a happy thought to reprefent the dead children by little cherubs ho-
vering in the air ; if the picture had had an *em-
blematical* caft. In *ferious portrait*, the thought
feems rather out of place.

At Wilton-houfe the accomplifhed Sir Philip Sidney (whofe beloved fifter was married to
the Earl of Pembroke) wrote his Arcadia; a
work of fuch fancy, that although not accom-
modated to the refinement of this age, it was
greatly admired in the laft, and went rapidly
through eight editions.

* By the late Lord Orford.

SECT. IX.

FROM Wilton we returned to Saliſbury; and from thence proceeded to Fonthill, the ſeat of Mr. Beckford. The road conveyed us through lanes, along the edge of the plain. About Denton the ground lay beautifully; the hills deſcending gently on each ſide.

Fonthill is a noble houſe, ſituated in a park, which contains great variety of ground. It takes its name from a woody hill and fountain hard by it, from which riſes a ſtream that aſſiſts in forming an artificial river, decorated by a very ſumptuous bridge. If the bridge had been more ſimple, the ſcene about it would have been more pleaſing. The ground, though *artificially formed, ſlopes well* to the river on each ſide, and beyond the bridge opens into a ſweet retiring valley.

Mr. Beckford ſeems alſo to have been aſſiduous in making a collection of pictures; and in point of numbers, he has ſucceeded. A Socrates, by Salvator, is moſt eſteemed. But though a capital picture, it ſeems ill-coloured, being a mere yellowiſh clair obſcure; nor has Socrates any character. I muſt add, however, that

that I have, oftener than once, judged falfely on the firft fight of Salvator's pictures, which have pleafed me more on a fecond view. This, however, is certainly a fault. We expect from a good picture, as from a good man, a favourable impreffion at fight.

But if there be few good pictures at Fonthill, there is abundance of fplendor ; not without a little dafh of vanity and oftentation. What is wanting in tafte, is made up in finery. Never houfe was fo bedecked with all the pride of upholftery. The very plate-glafs in one room coft fifteen hundred pounds*.

From Fonthill we proceeded through Hendon to Stourhead, the feat of Mr. Hoare, along downs overlooking an extenfive diftance on the left. We foon came in fight of the houfe and plantations, adorned with towers ftretching in a line along the horizon. The plantations, which feemed to ftand on a flat, appeared, in this diftant view, very regular, and

---

* Since this was written, I have been informed that Fonthill hath been much improved ; particularly that a cathedral hath been built of the full dimenfions of a genuine one. As Mr. Wyatt was the architect, it muft be a noble edifice ; and if it be properly ftationed, it muft be a grand decoration.

gave

gave us but an unfavourable idea of the place. The myftery, however, of this apparently un-pleafing fituation, was unravelled when we came upon the fpot.

Mr. Hoare purchafed Stourhead about forty years ago, of Lord Stourton, who takes his title from a village of that name in the neigh-bourhood. The improved grounds confift of three parallel vallies; all of them clofed at one end by an immenfe terrace, running feveral miles in length, with little deviation either to the right or left. This was the horizontal ftretch of unpleafing ground, which we faw at a diftance. The vallies run from it nearly at right angles; and were entirely fkreened from the eye, as we approached.

But though Mr. Hoare has taken all the three vallies, confifting of feveral miles in cir-cumference, within his improvements, he has *adorned* that only which lies neareft his houfe. The other two are planted and cut into rides; but the wood is yet young.

The houfe is built on an elegant defign by Colin Campbell, the architect of Wanftead-houfe in Effex. It confifts of a bafement; one grand floor, and an attic. We enter a handfome hall, and pafs into the faloon, which

is

is a noble room, fixty feet in length. On each fide of thefe rooms range the apartments.

Several good pictures adorn them. Thofe we admired moft, were

Some Market peafants, by Gainfborough. Both the figures and the effect of this picture are pleafing.

The Conference between Jacob and Efau, by Rofa of Tivoli. This is a capital picture, and abounds with amufement, though it is neither painted in the mafter's beft manner, nor are the figures well-grouped.

A fmall landfcape, by Lucatelli.

A Holy Family, by Caracci.

A landfcape, by Rembrandt. The back-ground and fky are dark; and the figures fitting on the fore-ground, and feen by fire-light, have a good effect.

A Baptift's Head in a Charger, by Carlo Dolci.

A good copy of Reuben's Boys at Wilton.

Elifha reftoring the Widow's Son, by Rembrandt. This is efteemed the moft capital picture of the collection; but it wants a *whole*, and the prophet a *character*.

From the houfe we went to view the improvements around it. That valley near which

I 4   the

the houfe ftands, and which I have mentioned as the moft adorned, contains a very noble fcene. It is called the valley of *Six-wells*, from fix heads of the river Stour, which arife here, and which the Stourton family take for their arms. The produce of thefe fprings is collected into a grand piece of water; in which, and the improvements on its banks, confift the beauties of the fcene.

In the common round, we are carried firft to the lower parts, along the margin of the lake, which we crofs in a narrow part, by a fuperb wooden bridge, and ftill continuing along the water, are amufed with a grotto, which has more propriety in it, than thefe places commonly have. Here arifes one of the heads of the Stour, which a well-cut river God (Deus ipfe loci) pours from his urn.

There is another grotto alfo near this, in which the fprings are collected into a marble bath. It is adorned with the ftatue of a fleeping nymph, under whom you read thefe lines:

Nymph of the grot, thefe facred ftreams I keep,
And to the murmur of thefe waters fleep.
Ah! fpare my flumbers; gently tread the cave;
And drink in filence; or in filence lave.

Leaving

Leaving thefe grottos, we afcend the higher grounds, and fo proceed from one ornamental building to another, every where entertained with different views of the lake, and its banks.

One of thefe buildings is very beautiful. It is called the Pantheon, as it is built on fome-thing like the model of the Pantheon at Rome. Though it is only the *ornament of a garden*, it is a *fplendid edifice*. The rotunda, which is the grand part of it, is lighted from the top, and is thirty-fix feet in diameter. To this is added a portico, and an apartment on each fide. The infide of the rotunda is adorned with ftatues and bas-relievos; and in the centre ftands an excellent Hercules, by Ryfbrach.

This ftatue was the work of emulation. Ryfbrach had long enjoyed the public favour without a rival. Schemaker firft arofe as a competitor; and afterwards Rubiliac, both artifts of great merit; the latter of uncommon abilities. Ryfbrach, piqued at feeing the ap-plaufe of the public divided, executed this fta-tue as a proof of his fkill. He compofed it from the felected limbs of fix or feven of the heroes of Broughton's amphitheatre; a fcene

of

of diverfion, at that time, in high repute. The brawny arms were taken from that chief him-felf; the cheft from the *coachman*, a champion well known in his day by that appellation; and the legs from Ellis the painter, who took more delight in Broughton's amphitheatre, than in his own painting-room.

Having finifhed our circuit round the gar-den, we were on the whole much pleafed. There is a greatnefs in the *defign*, though fome-times a littlenefs in the *execution*. The build-ings, in general, are good; but they are too nu-merous and too fumptuous. The gilt-crofs is a very difgufting object. Indeed, fimplicity is every where too much wanting. Many of the open-ings alfo are forced; and the banks of the lake in fome places formal; the paths are mere zig-zags; the going off of the water, and all the ma-nagement about the head of the lake, which is always a bufinefs difficult to manage, is awk-ward and perplexed; and as to the grounds near the houfe, they are ftill in the old ftyle of avenues and viftas. We faw many things at the fame time which pleafed us, particularly the *line of the lake*, in general, along its fhores; the woody fkreens that environed it; and the

effect

effect of some of the buildings in the landscape, *when seen single*, especially that of the Pantheon. On the whole, we spent an agreeable summer evening at Stourhead, and found more amusement than we generally find in places so highly adorned.

The next morning we visited the more distant parts of Mr. Hoare's improvements, the other two vallies and the terrace. The vallies will be more beautiful, as the woods improve; at present they are but unfurnished; and yet in their naked state we saw more clearly the peculiarity of the ground. Three vallies, thus closed by an immense terrace, is a singular production of nature. Some parts of the terrace command a most extensive distance. At the point of it, where it falls into the lower ground, a triangular tower is erected for the sake of the view. Over the door is the figure of King Alfred, with this inscription:

In

In Memory of Alfred the Great,
Who, on this fummit,
Erected his Standard
Againſt Daniſh Invaders.
He inſtituted Juries;
Eſtabliſhed a Militia;
Created and exerted
A Naval Force:
A Philoſopher and a Chriſtian;
The Father of his People;
The Founder
Of the Engliſh Monarchy,
And of Liberty.

From the tower of Alfred, we returned to Stourhead, after a ride of at leaſt eight miles through the different parts of Mr. Hoare's plantations.

S E C T. X.

FROM Stourhead to Froom, we paſſed through an incloſed country, which is barren of amuſement. On our right, we left Maiden-Bradley, an old houſe belonging to the Duke of Somerſet; and went a few miles out of our road to ſee Longleat, the manſion of Lord Weymouth.

Longleat is a noble old fabric, the workmanſhip of John Padua, about the year 1567. This architect was much eſteemed by the Protector Somerſet, whoſe houſe in the Strand he built. Sir John Thyn, who employed him here, was one of the Protector's principal officers. The ſtyle, however, of Longleat has more a caſt of the Gothic, than that of Somerſet-Houſe, which makes a nearer approach to Grecian architecture *. Neither poſſeſſes enough of its reſpective ſtyle, to be beautiful in its kind. The Gothic ſtyle perhaps at beſt is but ill adapted to private buildings. We

---

* Somerſet-Houſe in the Strand is now pulled down, and an expenſive edifice for various offices erected in its room.

chiefly

chiefly admire it, when its clustered pillars adorn the walls of some cathedral; when its pointed ribs spread along the roof of an aisle; or when the tracery of a window occupies the whole end of a choir. Gothic ornaments in this style of magnificence lose their littleness. They are not considered as *parts*, but are lost in *one vast whole*; and contribute only to impress a *general* idea of richness.

We sometimes indeed see the *smaller appendages* of cathedrals decorated very beautifully in the Gothic style; as the chapter-house at Salisbury, and that most elegant building at Ely, called the *Parish-church*. But in these buildings the *proportions* chiefly fill the eye: for which such ornaments are contrived, as have a good effect. Ornaments of this kind I have never seen used in any *private house* of Gothic construction. Nor indeed are they proper. As they are only found in sacred buildings, it might perhaps have been esteemed a mode of profaneness, to adopt them in private structures. This idea, indeed, the Gothic architects themselves seem to have had, by never using them but in churches.

On the whole, the Grecian architecture seems much better adapted to a private dwell-

7   ing-

ing-houfe, than the Gothic. It has a better *affortment*, if I may fo fpeak, of proper ornaments, and proportions for all its purpofes. The Gothic ornaments might drefs up a hall or a faloon; but they could do little more: we fhould find it difficult to decorate the flat roof of an apartment with them, or a paffage, or a ftair-cafe.

Nor are the *conveniencies*, which the Grecian architecture beftows on *private buildings*, lefs confiderable, than the beauty of its *decorations*. The Gothic palace is an *incumbered* pile. We are amufed with looking into thefe manfions of antiquity, as objects of curiofity; but fhould never think of comparing them in point of convenience with the great houfes of modern tafte, in which the hall and the faloon fill the eye on our entrance; are noble refervoirs for air; and grand antichambers to the feveral rooms of ftate that divide on each hand from them.

Longleat has nothing of the Grecian grandeur to recommend it. It is a large fquare building, with a court in the middle; which is intended to enlighten the inner chambers. The whole is certainly a grand pile; but it has little beauty, and I fhould fuppofe lefs convenience.

nience. It is at prefent however exceedingly in difhabille, and the furniture feems to be the relics of the laft century. The family of the Thynnes cover the walls in great profufion. We rarely fee fo numerous a collection of portraits without one that is able to fix the eye.

Be the infide of the houfe and its contents however what they may, when we view it feated, as it is, in the centre of a noble park, which flopes down to it in all directions, itfelf a grand object, evidently the capital of thefe wide domains, it has certainly a very princely appearance.

Somewhere among the woods of this manfion, was firft naturalized the Weymouth-pine. This fpecies of pine is among the moft formal of its brotherhood; and yet the planter muft confider it, in point of variety, as an acquifition. The patriarch-pine, Mr. Walpole tells us, ftill exifts, but we did not fee it.

SECT. XI.

FROM Longleat we purfued our road through Froom to Wells. The firft part of our journey prefented nothing very interefting. As we approached Mendip-hills, the road divides ; one branch leading *over* thofe high grounds, the other *under* them. We chofe the latter, which afforded us, on the right, thofe hills for a back-ground ; and on the left, an extenfive diftance, in which Glaftonbury-tor, as it is called, is the moft confpicuous feature.

Our approach to Wells, from the *natural* and *incidental* beauties of the fcene, was uncommonly picturefque. It was a hazy evening ; and the fun, declining low, was hid behind a deep purple cloud, which covered half the hemifphere, but did not reach the weftern horizon. Its lower fkirts were gilt with dazzling fplendor, which fpread downwards, not in diverging rays, but in one uniform ruddy glow ; and uniting at the bottom with the

K   mif-

miftinefs of the air, formed a rich, yet modeft
tint, with which Durcote-hill, projecting boldly
on the left, the towers of Wells beyond it, and
all the objects of the diftance, were tinged;
while the foreground, feen againft fo bright a
piece of fcenery, was overfpread with the
darkeft fhades of evening. The whole together invited the pencil, without foliciting the
imagination. But it was a tranfitory fcene.
As we ftood gazing at it, the fun funk below
the cloud, and being ftripped of all its fplendor
by the hazinefs of the atmofphere, fell, like a
ball of fire, into the horizon; and the whole
radiant vifion faded away.

Wells is a pleafant town, and agreeably fituated. The cathedral is a beautiful pile, notwithftanding it is of Saxon architecture. The
front is exceedingly rich, and yet the parts are
large. In the towers, the upper ftories are
plain, and make a good contraft with the richnefs of the lower. But this circumftance appears to moft advantage when the towers are
feen in profile; in front there is too much ornament. In the infide the Saxon heavinefs
prevails more. The choir-part is in better
tafte; and the retiring pillars of the chapel beyond

yond the communion-table, produce an unufual and very pleafing effect, like that at Salifbury. The chapter-houfe is an elegant octagon, fupported by a fingle pillar. One of the
parifh churches alfo at Wells is adorned with
a very handfome Gothic tower, and is itfelf a
beautiful pile.

Near Wells is a famous cavern, called Okey-
hole. It lies under Mendip-hills, which in
this place form a beautiful recefs, adorned with
rock and wood. A recefs of this kind appears
of little value to thofe who are acquainted with
mountainous countries; but in the fouth of
England it is a novel fcene. As to the cavern
itfelf, it runs about three huudred yards under
ground, dividing into three large apartments.
But no cavern that I know, except that at
Caftleton in Derbyfhire *, is worth vifiting in
a picturefque light. Caverns, in general, are
mere holes, and have no connection with the
ground about them. That at Caftleton has a
grand entrance, and the rocky fcenery, with
which it is hung, forms a moft magnificent
approach. But in the cavern here, there is no

---

* See an account of it in Mr. G.'s Northern Tour, vol. ii.
p. 210.

gran-

grandeur of this kind; fo that it contributes little to the beauty of the recefs in which it lies.

From Okey-hole we returned to Wells; and from thence proceeded to Glaftonbury; the ruins of which had highly raifed our expectation.

S E C T. XII.

THE ground on which the abbey of Glaſtonbury ſtands, is higher than the neighbouring diſtrict, which is a perfect flat; info-
much, that tradition ſays, it was formerly covered with the ſea. If that was the caſe, the
ground which the abbey occupies, if not an
iſland, was at leaſt a peninſula. To this day it
bears the name of *the Iſle of Avelon*; and the
meadows around it ſeem plainly to have been
waſhed and relinquiſhed by the ſea.

·The abbey of Glaſtonbury, therefore, does
not enjoy that choice ſituation which the generality of religious houſes poſſeſs. *Original
foundations*, like this, were generally fixed by
accidental cauſes. An eſcape from a ſhipwreck ;
a battle ; a murder; the ſcene of ſome prince's
death ; with a variety of other circumſtances,
have commonly determined their ſite ; ſo that
if they enjoy a good ſituation, it ſeems to be
accidental. Thoſe religious houſes whoſe ſituation we particularly admire, I ſhould conjecture, have been chiefly colonies, or off-ſets

K 3   from

from the great religious houses. In *these* there might be a *choice of situation*.

The event which settled the situation of this abbey, is firmly attested, on the proof of Romish legends. When Joseph of Aremathea came to preach the Gospel in Britain, as it is asserted he did, he landed on the Isle of Avelon; and fixing his staff in the ground, (a dry thorn-saplin, which had been his companion through all the countries he had passed,) fell asleep. When he awoke, he found, to his great surprise, that his staff had taken root, and was covered with white blossoms. From this miracle, however, he drew a very natural conclusion, that as the use of his staff was thus taken from him, it was ordained that he should fix his abode in this place. Here, therefore, he built a chapel, which, by the piety of succeeding times, increased into this magnificent foundation.

Of this immense fabric nothing now remains, but a part of the *great church*, *St. Joseph's chapel*, an *old gate-way*, part of the *abbot's lodge*, and the *kitchen*.

Of the *great church*, the south side is nearly entire; some part of the east end remains; a little of the crofs ifle; and a remnant of the tower;

all

all of the pureft and moft elegant Gothic.
The north fide was lately taken down, and the
materials were applied to build a meeting-
houfe. From this defalcation, however, the
ruin, as a picturefque object, feems to have
fuffered little. In *correfpondent* parts, if one
only be taken away, or confiderably fractured,
it may poffibly be an advantage. But we
greatly regret the lofs of the weft end, which
was taken down to build a town-hall. Still
more we regret the lofs of the tower; as the
eye wants fome elevated part to give an apex
to the whole. Befides, in that part of the
tower which remains, there is rather a formality. Two fimilar points, which have been
the fhoulders of a Gothic arch, arife in equal
dimenfions, and do not eafily fall into a picturefque form.

St. Jofeph's chapel, which ftands near the
weft end of the great church, is almoft entire.
The roof indeed is gone; but the walls have
fuffered little dilapidation. This chapel was
probably more ancient than the church, as it
has evidently a mixture in it of Saxon architecture ; but the ftyle is very pure in its kind ;
and the whole is rich and beautiful. It is no
little addition to its beauty, that ivy is fpread

about

about over the walls, in fuch juft proportion, as to adorn without defacing them.

On the fouth-weft of St. Jofeph's chapel, ftands the *Gate of ftrangers*, which feems to have been a heavy building, void of elegance and beauty. Not far from the Gate of ftrangers, and connected with it in defign, are fhewn the foundations of the Linguift's lodge: but no part of it, unlefs it be a poftern, is now left. This was a very neceffary part of an endowment, which was vifited by ftrangers from all parts of the world.

The *Abbot's lodge* has been a large building. It ranges parallel with the fouth fide of the church; and was nearly entire within the memory of man. It was a fuit of feven apartments on a floor; but very little of it is now left. In the year 1714 it was taken down to anfwer fome purpofe of economy, though it feems never to have been a ftructure of any beauty.

Hard by the Abbot's lodge ftands the *Kitchen*, which is to this day very entire, and is both a curious remnant of antiquity, and a noble monument of monkifh hofpitality. It is a fquare building, calculated to laft for ages. Its walls are four feet thick, and yet ftrengthened with

maffy

maſſy buttreſſes. They have, indeed, an im-
menſe roof to ſupport, which is ſtill in excellent repair. It is conſtructed of ſtone, and
ſeems to be a work of very curious maſonry,
running up in the form of an octagonal pyra-
mid, and finiſhed at the top in a double cupola.
The under part of this cupola received the ſmoke,
in channels along the inſide of the roof; and
the upper part contained a bell, which firſt
called the ſociety to dinner, and afterwards the
neighbouring poor to alms. The inſide of the
Kitchen is an octagon; four chimnies taking
off the corners of the ſquare. It has two doors,
and meaſures twenty-two feet from one to the
other, and a hundred and ſeventy from the
bottom to the top. In this Kitchen, it is recorded, that twelve oxen were dreſſed generally every week, beſides a proportional quantity of other victuals.

Theſe are all the viſible remains of this great
houſe. Foundations are traced far and wide,
where, it is conjectured, the cloiſters ran; the
monks cells; the ſchools; the dormitories;
halls; and other offices. The whole together has
been an amazing combination of various buildings. It had the appearance indeed of a conſiderable town, containing perhaps the largeſt ſociety

ciety under one government, and the moſt extenſive foundation that ever appeared in England in any form. Its fraternity is ſaid to have
conſiſted of five hundred eſtabliſhed monks,
beſides nearly as many retainers on the abbey.
Above four hundred children were not only
educated in it, but entirely maintained. Stran-
gers from all parts of Europe were liberally received ; claſſed according to their ſex and nation ; and might conſider the hoſpitable roof,
under which they lodged, as their own. Five
hundred travellers, with their horſes, (though
they generally, I ſhould ſuppoſe, travelled on
foot,) have been lodged at once within its walls.
While the poor from every ſide of the country
waited the ringing of the alms-bell ; when they
flocked in crowds, young and old, to the gate
of the monaſtery, where they received, every
morning, a plentiful proviſion for themſelves and
their families: all this appears great and noble.

On the other hand, when we conſider five
hundred perſons, bred up in indolence, and
loſt to the commonwealth ; when we conſider
that theſe houſes were the great nurſeries of
ſuperſtition, bigotry, and ignorance ; the ſtews
of ſloth, ſtupidity, and perhaps intemperance ;
when we conſider, that the education received
in

in them had not the leaft tincture of ufeful
learning, good manners, or true religion, but
tended rather to vilify and difgrace the human
mind ; when we confider that the pilgrims and
ftrangers who reforted thither, were idle vaga-
bonds, who got nothing abroad that was equi-
valent to the occupations they left at home;
and when we confider, laftly, that indifcrimi-
nate alms-giving is not real charity, but an
avocation from labour and induftry, checking
every idea of exertion, and filling the mind
with abject notions, we are led to acquiefce in
the fate of thefe great foundations, and view
their ruins, not only with a picturefque eye,
but with moral and religious fatisfaction.

This great houfe poffeffed the ampleft reve-
nues of any religious houfe in England. Its
ancient domains are fuppofed *now* to yield not
lefs than an annual income of two hundred
thoufand pounds. I have heard them calculated at much more.

Within a mile of the abbey ftands the *Torr*,
which is by much the higheft land in the
ifland of Avelon, and had been our land-mark
through an approach of many leagues. The
fummit of this hill is decorated with a ruin,
which has its effect, though in itfelf it poffeffes

no beauty.   It is a ſtructure of ambiguous intention.   One tradition ſuppoſes it to have
been a ſea-mark, for which it is well adapted.
Another makes it an oratory.   To the abbot
it certainly belonged.

Here the holy man, when Satan led him
aſide, might ſometimes aſcend, and looking
round him, might ſee all the country his own;
houſes and villages filled with his vaſſals; meadows covered with innumerable flocks and
herds to ſupport the ſtrength of his table;
rivers and woods abounding with fiſh and
game to furniſh its delicacies; fields waving
with corn to fill his granaries and his cellars;
and, among other ſources of luxury, no fewer
than ſeven ample parks, well ſtocked with ve-
niſon.   Here was a glorious view indeed! His
heart might dilate, as the viſion expanded: and
if he were not well upon his guard, he might
eaſily have miſtaken an earthly reverie for holy
joy and religious gratitude.

Near the bottom of this hill are found great
quantities of that ſpecies of putrefaction which
reſembles a coiled ſerpent; or, as it is often
called, an *Ammon's horn*.

The ruins of Glaſtonbury-abbey occupy a
piece of ground, about a mile in circumference,

rence, which has no peculiar beauty, but might be improved into a very grand scene, if it were judiciously planted, and laid out with just so much art, as to discover the ruins to the best advantage. But such schemes of improvement are calculated only for posterity. A young plantation would ill accord with such antique accompaniments. The oak would require at least a century's growth, before its moss-grown limbs could be congenial with the ruins it adorned.

I should ill deserve the favours I met with from the learned antiquarian, who has the care of these ruins, though he occupies only the humble craft of a shoemaker, if I did not attempt to do some justice to his zeal and piety. No picturesque eye could more admire these venerable remains for their beauty, than he did for their sanctity. Every stone was the object of his devotion. But above all the appendages of Glastonbury, he reverenced most the famous thorn which sprang from St. Joseph's staff, and blossoms at Christmas. On this occasion he gave us the following relation.

It was at that time, he said, when the King resolved to alter the common course of the year, that he first felt distress for the honour of the

the houfe of Glaftonbury. If the time of Chriftmas were changed, who could tell how the credit of this miraculous plant might be af-fected ? In fhort, with the fortitude of a Jewifh feer, he ventured to expoftulate with the King upon the fubject; and informed his Majefty, in a letter, of the difgrace that might poffibly enfue, if he perfifted in his defign of altering the natural courfe of the year. But though his confcience urged him upon this bold action, he could not but own the flefh trembled. He had not the leaft doubt, he faid, but the King would immediately fend down an order to have him hanged. He pointed to the fpot where the laft abbot of Glaftonbury was executed for not furrendering his abbey; and he gave us to underftand, there were men now alive who could fuffer death, in a good caufe, with equal fortitude. His zeal, however, was not put to this fevere trial. The King was more merciful than he expected; for though his Majefty did not follow his advice, it never appeared that he took the leaft offence at the freedom of his letter.

The death of the laft abbot of Glaftonbury is indeed a mournful tale, as it is reprefented by the writers of thofe times, and was cal-culated

culated to make a lasting impression on the country.

This abbot is said to have been a pious and good man; careful of his charge, kind to the poor, and exemplary in his conduct. He is particularly mentioned as a man of great temperance; which, in a cloister, was not, perhaps, at that day, the reigning virtue. What was still as uncommon, he was a lover of learning; and not only took great care of the education of those young men, who were brought up in his house, but was at the expence of maintaining several of them at the universities. He was now very old, and very infirm; and having passed all his life in his monastery, knew little more of the world than he had seen within its walls.

It was the misfortune of this good abbot to live in the tyrannical days of Henry VIII., and at that period when the suppression of monasteries was his favourite object. Henry had applied to many of the abbots, and by threats and promises had engaged several of them to surrender their trusts. But the abbot of Glastonbury, attached to his house, and connected with his fraternity, refused to surrender. He was conscious of his own innocence; and thought guilt only

only had to fear from the inquifition that was abroad. But Henry, whofe haughty and imperious fpirit, unufed to control, foared above the trifling diftinctions between innocence and guilt, was highly incenfed; and determined to make an example of the abbot of Glaftonbury to terrify others. An order firft came down for him to appear forthwith before the council. The difficulties of taking fo long a journey, appeared great to an old man, who had feldom travelled beyond the limits of his monaftery. But as there was no redrefs, he got into an eafy horfe-litter, and fet out. In his mode of travelling, we fee the ftate and dignity, which certainly required fome correction, of the great ecclefiaftics of that age. His retinue, it is faid, confifted of not fewer than an hundred and fifty horfemen.

The King's fending for him, however, was a mere pretext. The real purpofe was to prevent his fecreting his effects; as it was never intended that he fhould return. Proper perfons, therefore, were commiffioned to fearch his apartments in his abfence, and fecure the wealth of the monaftery. His fteward, in the mean-time, who was a gentleman of the degree of a Knight, was corrupted to make what difcoveries he could.

could. It was an eafy matter in thofe days to procure evidence, where it was already determined to convict. In one of the abbot's cabinets fome ftrictures upon the divorce were either found, or pretended to be found. Nothing elfe could be obtained againft him.

During this interval, the abbot, who knew nothing of thefe proceedings, waited on the council. He was treated refpectfully; and informed, that the King would not *force* any man to do what he wifhed him to *do freely.* However, as his Majefty intended to receive his final determination on the fpot, he was at liberty to return.

Being thus difmiffed, the abbot thought all was now over, and that he might be permitted to end his days peaceably in his beloved monaftery.

He was now nearly at the end of his journey, having arrived at Wells, which is within five miles of Glaftonbury, when he was informed, that a county-court (of what kind is not fpecified) was convened there on that day, to which he, as abbot of Glaftonbury, was fummoned. He went into the court room accordingly; and as his ftation required, was going to take his place at the upper end of it, among

L   the

the principal gentry of the country; when the crier called him to the bar, where he was accufed of high treafon.

The old man, who had not the leaft conception of the affair, was utterly aftonifhed; and turning to his fteward, who ftood near him, afked, if he knew what could be the meaning of all this? That traitor, whifpering in his ear, wifhed him not to be caft down, for he knew the meaning of it was only to terrify him into a compliance. Though the court, therefore, on the evidence of the paper taken out of his cabinet, found him guilty of high treafon, he had ftill no idea of what was intended. From the court he was conveyed to his litter, and conducted to Glaftonbury; ftill in fufpence how all this would end.

When he arrived under the walls of his abbey, the litter was ordered to ftop; and an officer riding up to him, bad him prepare for inftant death. A prieft, at the fame time, prefented himfelf to take his confeffion.

The poor old abbot, utterly confounded at the fuddennefs of the thing, was quite unmanned. He begged with tears, and for God's fake, they would allow him fome little time for recollection. But his tears were vain.

Might

Might he not then juſt enter his monaſtery;
take leave of his friends ; and recommend himſelf tò their prayers ? All was to no purpoſe.
He was dragged out of his litter, and laid upon
a hurdle, to which a horſe being yoked, he
was drawn along the ground to the Torr,
and there, to make the triumph complete, was
hung up, in his monk's habit, and in ſight of
his monaſtery. It was a triumph, however,
that was attended with the tears and lamenta-
tions of the whole country, which had long
conſidered this pious man, as a friend, benefactor, and father.

How far this ſhocking ſtory, in all its circumſtances of ſtrange precipitancy, and wanton
cruelty, may be depended on, conſidering the
hands through which it is conveyed, may be
matter of doubt : thus much, however, is certain, that if the picture here given of the royal
ſavage of thoſe days be not an exact portrait, it
bears evidently a ſtriking reſemblance.

S E C T. XIII.

HAVING given a laſt look at the picturesque ruins of Glaſtonbury, we left them
with regret. That pure ſtyle of Gothic, in
which this grand houſe was compoſed, it is
probable, gave the key-tone in architecture to
all the churches in this neighbourhood; for it
is certain a better taſte prevails among them,
as far as we obſerved, than in any other part of
England through which we had travelled.

From Glaſtonbury we took the road to
Bridgewater, and paſſed through a very fine
country.

About three miles beyond Piper's Inn, we
mounted a grand natural terrace, called the
heights of Pontic.

On the right we had the whole range of
Mendip hills, which, though inconſiderable in
themſelves, made ſome figure in this view,
with pleaſant ſavannahs ſtretching among them.
Beyond the hills appeared the ſea, and the
iſland of Steep-holms. The nearer grounds,
between this diſtance and the eye, were filled

2   with

with ample woods, which ranged, not in patches
here and there difperfed, but in one extended
furface of tufted foliage; for we faw little more
from the heights on which we ftood, than the
varied tops of the woods beneath us. The
whole country, I believe, is a fcene of cultivation; and the woods little more, in fact, than
hedge-rows. But one row fucceeding another,
the intermediate fpaces are concealed, together
with all the regularity of that mode of plant-
ing; and the whole appears, in the diftance, as
one vaft bed of foliage.

On the left we had the fame kind of country; only the hills on this fide of Pontic are
much fuperior to thofe of Mendip on the other.
Among the favannahs on this fide, fhoot the
extenfive plains of Sedgmore, which ftretch
far and wide before the eye. Here the unfortunate Monmouth tried his caufe with his
uncle James; and all the country was afterwards the fcene of thofe acts of brutality, which
Kirk and Jefferies committed, and which are
ftill remembered with horror and deteftation.

This vaft diftance, which we furveyed from
the heights of Pontic, not only filled the eye
with its grandeur as a whole, but was every
where interfperfed with amufing objects, which

L 3   adorned

adorned its feveral divifions. In one part
Lord Chatham's obelifk pointed out the domains of Pynfent. In another part we were
told, the rich fcenes before us were the woods
of Sir Charles Tint. The tall fpire which
arofe on the right belonged to the great
church at Bridgewater; and the feveral little
fpots of water, glittering under the fun-beams,
were reaches of the river Parret,

> Inlaying, as with molton-glafs, the vale,
> That fpread beyond the fight.——

At the diftance at which we ftood, we could
not well unite all thefe bright fpots of the river
into a winding courfe; but the imagination
eafily traced the union.

The diftances, indeed, from the heights of
Pontic, are both grand and picturefque; picturefque, when thus reduced into parts; though
in their immenfity greatly too extenfive for
painting. The whole fcene was a tranflation
of a paffage in Virgil, bringing before our
eyes,

> ——Mare velivolum, terrafque jacentes,
> Littoraque, et latos populos.——

We have the fame view elfewhere:

> ——From the mountain's ridge,
> O'er tufted tops of intervening woods,
> Regions on regions blended in the clouds.

I can-

I cannot forbear contrasting this grand view with a few bold strokes of distance, which Moses gives us, when he tells us, " he went up " from the plains of Moab to the top of Pis- " gah; from whence the Lord shewed him all " the land of Gilead unto Dan, and all Naph- " tali, and the land of Ephraim and Manasseh, " and all the land of Judah, unto the utmost " sea; and on the south the plain of the valley " of Jericho unto Zoar."

On Mr. Hoare's terrace we had seen the spot where Alfred the Great mustered his scattered troops to oppose the Danes. The country near Bridgewater affords a scene, where, on another occasion, he appeared in a different character.

Where the Thone and the Parret join their waters, they form between them a piece of ground, containing about two acres, which is called the Isle of Athelney. In Saxon times it was not only surrounded by water, but with woods and marshes to a great extent, and was in every part of very difficult access. Here the gallant Alfred retired in his distresses, when he fled before the Danes, after the battle of Wilton. At first he considered it only as a place of refuge, and sustained himself by shoot-

L 4   ing

ing the wild deer with his arrows. But by degrees getting together a few of his friends, he fortified the ifland, and particularly the only avenue that led to it. From hence he often made fuccefsful inroads upon the Danifh quarters; and retreating among the marfhes, eluded purfuit. From hence too, in the habit of a minftrel, he made that celebrated excurfion to their camp, in which, under the pretence of amufing them with his fongs and buffooneries, he took an exact furvey of their fituation. He then laid his meafures fo judicioufly, and fell upon them with fo much well-directed fury, that he entirely broke their power during the remainder of his reign. In after-times, when fuccefs had crowned his enterprizes, he founded a monaftery in the ifland, in memory of the protection it had once afforded him. But its fite, which had nothing to recommend it, except this perfonal circumftance, was in all refpects fo inconvenient, that it never flourifhed, though it exifted till the times of the diffolution.

S E C T. XIV.

THERE is very little in Bridgewater, which was our next ftage, worth a traveller's attention. Its great boaft is the celebrated Blake, one of Cromwell's admirals, who was born in this town, and reprefented it in feveral parliaments.

The name of Blake can hardly occur to an Englifhman without fuggefting refpect. If ever any man was a *lover of his country*, without being actuated by *party*, or *any other finifter motive*, it was Blake. Whether in a divided commonwealth, one fide or the other fhould be *cordially chofen* by every citizen, is a nice queftion. Some of the ancient moralifts have held the affirmative. But a man may fee fuch errors on both fides, as may render a choice difficult. This feems to have been Blake's cafe. The *glory of his country* therefore was the only part he efpoufed. He fought, indeed, under Cromwell; but it was merely, he would fay, to *aggrandize Old England*. He often difliked the protector's politics. With the death

of

of Charles he was particularly difpleafed; and was heard to mutter, that to have faved the King's life, he would freely have ventured his own. But ftill he fought on; took an immenfe treafure from the Portuguefe; beat the Dutch in two or three defperate engagements; burnt the Dey of Tunis's fleet; awed the piratical States; and, above all, deftroyed the Spanifh plate-fleet in the harbour of Santa Cruz, which was thought a piece of the moft gallant feamanfhip that *ever* was performed. Some things in the mean time happened at home which he did not like, particularly Cromwell's treatment of the Parliament: but he ftill fought on; and would fay to his captains, *It is not for us to mind ftate matters, but to keep foreigners from fooling us.* What is fingular in this commander is, that all his knowledge in maritime affairs was acquired after he was fifty years of age. He had the theory of his profeffion, as it were, by intuition; and crowded as many gallant actions into nine or ten years, as might have immortalized as many commanders. One perfonal fingularity is recorded, which gives us a fort of portrait of him. When his choler was raifed, and he was bent on fome defperate undertaking, it was his cuftom to twirl his whif-

kers

kers with his fore-finger. Whenever that fign appeared, thofe about him well knew fomething dreadful was in agitation.

Such a *peculiarity*, however, could not eafily be made intelligible in a picture; and therefore it is more proper for *hiftory* than *reprefentation*. And yet I can conceive a portrait of Blake, in this attitude, if well managed, to have a good effect. His fleet might lie in the offing ready to fail. At a diftance might ftand a caftle, which he meant to attack, firing at his fleet, and involved in fmoke. Blake, with a few of his officers around him, might ftand on the fore-ground, occupying the principal part of the picture; and ready to embark in a boat, which was waiting for them on the ftrand. Blake himfelf might be reprefented in the attitude above defcribed, throwing a dreadful look at the caftle; but this dreadful look muft be in the hands of a mafter, or it will infallibly become grotefque and caricature. After all, though this difpofition might make a good picture, I know not that it would be intelligible enough to make a good portrait.

All this coaft, between Bridgewater and Briftol, is low, and fubject, in many parts, to overflowing tides. In the memorable ftorm

of

of November 1703, it was a melancholy fcene.
The fea broke over it with great outrage, and
did furprifing damage. In many places, as
you travel through it, you fee marks fet up by
the country people, to fhow how far the fea
poured in at that time. But, indeed, every
part of the Briftol channel is fubject to very
high tides at all times. In Bridgewater-river
it often rifes in an uncommon manner, and
comes forward in fuch rapid fwells, that it has
been known fometimes to overfet fhips. It
affects the river at Briftol alfo, and all the rivers
on the coaft; and, if I am not miftaken, on
the oppofite coaft likewife.

S E C T. XV.

AS we left Bridgewater, we drew nearer the
fea. In our way we paffed Sir Charles
Tint's plantations, which we had before feen
as parts of a diftance. They appeared now
ftretching to a great extent along the fide of a
hill, and beautifully interfperfed with lawns.
They were adorned with too many buildings,
which would, however, have had a better effect,
if they had not been painted white. A feat or
fmall building, painted white, may be an advantage in a view : but when thefe white fpots
are multiplied, the diftinction of their colour
detaches them from the other objects of the
fcene, with which they ought to combine :
they diftract the eye, and become feparate fpots,
inftead of parts of a whole.

In the neighbourhood of Sir Charles Tint's,
lies Enmore-caftle, the feat of Lord Egmont.
It is a new building, in the form of an old
caftle. A dry ditch furrounds it, which you
pafs

paſs by a draw-bridge. This carries you into a ſquare court, the four ſides of which are occupied by the apartments. It is called whimſical; and, no doubt, there is ſomething whimſical in the idea of a man's incloſing himſelf, in the reign of George the Second, in a fortreſs that would have ſuited the times of King Stephen. But if we can diveſt ourſelves of this idea, Enmore-caſtle ſeems to be a comfortable dwelling, in which there is contrivance and convenience. The ſituation of the ſtables ſeems the moſt whimſical. You enter them through a ſubterraneous paſſage, on the right of the great gate. There was no occaſion to carry the idea ſo far as to lock up the horſes within the caſtle. If the ſtables had been placed at ſome convenient diſtance, nobody, who ſhould even examine the caſtle under its antique idea, would obſerve the impropriety; while the inconvenience, as they are placed at preſent, is evident to every one who ſees them.

But if the houſe be well contrived within, it is certainly no picturefque object without. The towers, which occupy the corners and middle of the curtains, are all of equal height, which gives the whole an unpleaſing

appear-

appearance. If the tower at the entrance had been more elevated, with a watch-houfe at the top, in the manner of fome old caftles, the regularity might ftill have been obferved ; and the perfpective in every point, except exactly in the front, would have given the whole a more pleafing form.

But even with this addition, Enmore-caftle would be, in a picturefque light, only a very indifferent copy of its original. The old baronial caftle, in its ancient ftate, even before it had received from time the beauties of ruin, was certainly a more pleafing object than we have in this imitation of it. The *form* of Enmore is facrificed to *convenience*. To make the apartments regular within, the walls are regular without. Whereas our anceftors had no idea of uniformity. If one tower was fquare and low, the other, perhaps, would be round and lofty. The curtain too was irregular, following the declivity or projection of the hill on which it ftood. It was adorned alfo with watch-towers, here and there, at unequal diftances. Nor were the windows more regular, either in form or fituation, than the internal parts of the caftle, which they enlightened. Some jutting corner of a detached

hill

hill was alſo probably fortified with a projeƈt-
ing tower. A large buttreſs or two perhaps
propped the wall, in ſome part, where the attack of an enemy had made it weak: while
the *keep*, riſing above the caſtle, formed generally a grand apex to the whole. Amidſt all this
maſs of irregularity, the lines would be broken,
the light often beautifully received, and various points of view preſented, ſome of which
would be exceedingly piƈtureſque. WhereasEn-
more-caſtle, ſeen in every point of view, preſents a face of *unvaried ſameneſs*. Even taken
in perſpeƈtive, it affords no variety. We ſee
three ſimilar towers, with two ſimilar curtains
between them, on one ſide; and three ſimilar
towers, with two ſimilar curtains between
them, on the other. On the whole, therefore,
as it obtains no *particular convenience* from its
caſtle-form, and evidently no *particular beauty*,
it might, perhaps, have been as well if the noble founder had built, like other people, on a
modern plan.

S E C T. XVI.

FROM Enmore-caftle we afcended Quantoc-hills. Our views from the heights of Pontic were chiefly *inland*; but from the high grounds here, as we now approached the fea, we were entertained with beautiful coaft-views, which make a very agreable fpecies of landfcape.

The firft fcene of this kind was compofed of Bridgewater-bay, and the land around it. We faw indeed the two iflands of Flat-holms and Steep-holms, and the Welfh coaft beyond them; but they were wrapped in the ambiguity of a hazy atmofphere, which was of no advantage to the view. Hazinefs has often a good effect in a picturefque fcene. The variety of objects, fhapes, and hues which compofe an extenfive landfcape, though inharmonious in themfelves, may be harmonioufly united by one general tinge fpread over them. But here the land bore fo fmall a proportion to the water, that as we could not have a *picture*, and expected only *amufement*, we wifhed for more diftinctnefs.

M

tinctnefs. We had it foon; for before we left our ftation, a light breeze arifing from the weft fwept away the vapours: the diftant coaft became diftinct, and many a little white fail appeared in different parts of the channel, which had been loft before in obfcurity.

The *going off* of mifts and fogs is among the moft beautiful circumftances belonging to them. While the obfcurity is only *partially* clearing away, it often occafions a pleafing contraft between the *formed* and *unformed* parts of a landfcape; and like cleaning a dirty picture, pleafes the eye with feeing one part after another emerge into brightnefs. It has its effect alfo, when it goes off more fuddenly.

The exhibition we juft had of the fog's leaving the Welch coaft, was a *pleafing* one; but where there is a *coincidence of grand objects under fuch circumftances*, the exhibition is often *fublime*. One of the grandeft I remember to have met with was prefented at the late fiege of Gibraltar *.

It was near day-break on the 12th of April 1781, when a meffage was brought from the

* See Drinkwater's Journal.

3 fignal-

signal-houfe at the fummit of the rock, that the
long expected fleet, under Admiral Darby, was
in fight. Innumerable mafts were juft dif-
cerned from that lofty fituation; but could not
be feen from the lower parts of the caftle, being
obfcured by a thick fog, which had fet in from
the weft, and totally overfpread the opening of
the ftraits. In this uncertainty the garrifon
remained fome time; while the fleet, invefted
in obfcurity, moved flowly towards the caftle.
In the mean time, the fun becoming powerful,
the fog rofe like the curtain of a vaft theatre,
and difcovered *at once* the whole fleet, full and
diftinct before the eye. The convoy, confifting of near a hundred veffels, were in a compact body, led on by twenty-eight fail of the
line, and a number of tenders and other fmaller
veffels. A gentle wind juft filled their fails, and
brought them forward with a flow and folemn
motion. Had all this grand exhibition been
prefented *gradually*, the fublimity of it would
have been injured by the acquaintance the eye
would have made with it, during its approach;
but the appearance of it in all its greatnefs *at
once*, before the eye had examined the detail,
had a wonderful effect.

To this account of a grand effect from the clearing away of a fog, I fhall fubjoin another, which, though of the horrid kind, is grand and fublime in the higheft degree. It is taken from Captain Meares's voyage from China to the northern latitudes of America. That navigator, having gained the inhofpitable coaft he was in purfuit of, was failing among unknown bays and gulphs, when he was fuddenly immerfed in fo thick a fog, that the feamen could not even difcern an object from one end of the fhip to the other. Night too came on, which rendered every thing ftill more difmal. While the unhappy crew were ruminating on the variety of diftreffes that furrounded them, about midnight they were alarmed with the found of waves burfting and dafhing among rocks, within a little diftance of the head of the fhip. Inftantly turning the helm, they tacked about. But they had failed only a fhort way in this new direction, when they were terrified with the fame dreadful notes a fecond time. They altered their courfe again : but the fame tremendous found again recurred. At length day came on ; but the fog continuing as intenfe as before, they could fee nothing. All they knew was, that they were furrounded by rocks on

every

every fide; but how to efcape they had no
idea.   Once, during a momentary interruption
of the fog, they got a glimpfe of the fummit
of an immenfe cliff, covered with fnow, towering over the maft.   But the fog inftantly fhut
it in.   A more dreadful fituation cannot eafily
be conceived.   They had fteered in every direction, but always found they were land-
locked ;   and   though   they   were   continually
clofe to the fhore, on founding they could find
no bottom.   Their anchors therefore were of no
ufe.   Four days they continued in this dreadful
fufpence, tacking from fide to fide : on the 5th
the fog cleared away, and they had a view at
once of the terrors that furrounded them.
They had, by fome ftrange accident, found
their way into a bay, invironed on all fides
with precipices of immenfe height, covered
with fnow, and falling down to the water, in
lofty rocks, which were every where perpendicular, except in fome parts where the conftant
beating of the furge had hollowed them into
caverns.   The found they heard was from the
waters fwelling and rufhing into thefe caverns,
which abforbing them, drove them out again
with great fury againft the rocks at their
mouths, dafhing them into foam with a tre-

M 3   mendous

mendous found. Captain Meares now per-
ceived the paffage, through which he had been
driven into this fcene of horrors, and made his
efcape.

On reading fuch accounts as thefe in a picturefque light, one can hardly avoid making a
few remarks on the grand effects which may
often be produced by, what may be called, *the
fcenery of vapour.* Nothing offers fo extenfive
a field to the fancy in *invented* fcenes; nothing
fubjects even the *compofitions of nature* fo much
to the control and improvement of art. It
admits the painter to a participation with the
poet in the ufe of the machinery of *uncertain
forms*; to which both are indebted for their
fublimeft images. A *fublime image* is perhaps an
incorrect phrafe. The regions of fublimity are
not peopled by *forms*, but *hints*; they are not
enlightened by *funfhine*, but by *gleams* and
flafhes. The tranfient view of the fummit of a
cliff towering over the maft, filled the defpair-
ing feaman with more terror than if he had
feen the whole rocky bay. It fet his imagination at work. The ideas of *grace and beauty*
are as much raifed by leaving the image half
immerfed

immerſed in obſcurity, as the ideas of *terror*.
Definition, which throws a light on philoſophic
truth, deſtroys at once the airy ſhapes of fiction. Virgil has given more beauty in three
words,

—— Lumenque juventæ
Purpureum———

than he could have done in the moſt laboured
deſcription; as Grey likewiſe has in the two
following lines, though ſome cold critic would
probably aſk for an explanation:

O'er her warm cheek, and riſing boſom move
The bloom of young deſire, and purple light of love.

It is by ſnatches only that you catch a glimpſe
of ſuch beauties. Would you analyſe them,
the viſion diſſolves in the proceſs; and diſap-
pears, like life purſued to its laſt retreat by the
anatomiſt. You ruin the image by determining
its form, and identifying its tints.

As we proceeded farther along the heights
of Quantoc, we had views of the promontory
of Minehead, which forms a more beautiful
coaſt than Bridgewater-bay: the land is higher
and more varied. Here we had ſtill a diſtinct
view of the Briſtol channel, and the coaſt of

M 4 Wales.

Wales. The fea, as is not uncommon, happened to be beautifully variegated. It had a
reddifh hue with a tinge of rainbow green,
which being mixed together, formed different
gradations of kindred colours ; and fometimes
going off in purple, gave the furface of the
ocean a great refplendency.

Minehead feems by its fituation to confirm
what we were told, that its harbour was the
beft and fafeft in this part of the coaft. When
the great ftorm of 1703 ravaged all thefe fhores
with peculiar fury, Minehead was the only
harbour which could defend it's fhipping. It
is chiefly ufeful in the Irifh trade, as it lies in
the midway between Ireland and Briftol.

In fo ordinary a town as Watchet, we were
furprifed to find fo handfome a pier. But in
many of the ports along this coaft, though
inconfiderable in appearance, we fee a great
air of bufinefs. This little Mediterranean is
crowded with fkiffs paffing and repaffing ; and
has a brifk trade within itfelf in corn, metals,
lime-ftone, and other commodities. The coaft
about Watchet is very rocky ; and the crevices
of the rocks are curioufly veined with alabafter,
which

which makes a part of the traffic of the place. But the ftone from which the greateft advantage is derived, is a kind of pebble, found on the fhore, when the tide leaves it. Thefe pebbles burn into lime of fo peculiar a texture, that when placed under water, it affumes its original hardnefs. Even when pulverized, and laid upon land, it is turned into a kind of hard grit by the firft fhower of rain. In the foundation of bridges, therefore, and all ftone-work, which lies under water, the lime of Watchet is exceedingly valued. A fpecies of this kind of lime, Mr. Bryant informs us, was in ufe among the Romans: the foundation-ftones particularly of the great mole at Puteoli were united by this cement *.

From Watchet we purfued our route along the coaft. The promontory of Minehead ftill continued the principal feature of the view. As we approached it, a woody hill, which in the diftance adhered to the promontory, began more and more to detach itfelf from it: and as we came ftill nearer we difcovered a light airy building on its fummit, which by degrees ap-

* See Bryant's Differt. on the Wind Euroclydon, p. 17.

peared

peared to be an unfinished edifice with its scaffolding about it. In this condition it has probably a more picturesque effect than it will have, when it has completely taken the form which seems to be intended. At a distance it had the appearance of the Sibyl's temple at Tivoli: the tower is round, and the scaffolding annexed the idea of a range of ruined pillars supporting the roof.

As we turned a little from the sea, Dunster-castle, the seat of Mr. Lutterell, opened before us at about the distance of half a mile, and made a striking appearance. It is, indeed, on the whole, one of the grandest artificial objects we had met with on our journey. Its towers, which are picturesque, arise near the summit of a woody hill, which seems connected with another hill, much higher, though it is in fact detached from it. This apparent union makes the composition more agreable, and is of great advantage to the view. It takes away that idea of art which an insulated hill would be apt to raise. The consequence of this grand object is greatly increased by a *dead flat* between it and the eye. *Broken ground* in
itself

itſelf is more beautiful; but a *flat* often carries the eye more directly to a capital object, with which alſo it often very agreably contraſts. I ſpeak, however, undecidedly, becauſe ſome-times it is otherwiſe. But in the preſent caſe we thought the approach by a flat had a good effect.

From the terrace of the caſtle we had a great variety of amuſing landſcapes; though nothing very intereſting. We obtained a good idea, however, of the form of the country; and found that Dunſter-caſtle, which ſtands high, is ſurrounded, though at a conſiderable diſ-tance, by grounds that are much higher. In this amuſing circle round the walls of the caſtle, we had three diſtinct ſpecies of landſcape, a *park-ſcene*; a tract of *mountainous country*; and a *ſea-coaſt*.

In the time of the civil wars, Dunſter-caſtle had a reſpectable name; and was conſidered as one of the ſtrongeſt of the King's garriſons in the weſt. When his affairs were in the wane after the battle of Naiſby, it was fixed on as the beſt place of refuge for the Prince of Wales; but the plague immediately breaking out in the town of Dunſter, ſome other place of ſecurity was ſought for.

At

At Dunſter, we were told, there is a very elegant Gothic church, built in the time of Henry VII. when it is commonly ſuppoſed Gothic architecture was in its pureſt ſtate; though I think it was rather, as all arts end in refinement, at that period, on the decline. Whether this church, however, were of elegant architecture, or not, the late intelligence we received did not ſuffer us to examine. We had already left the place; and when there, had conceived the caſtle to be the only thing worth viſiting.

From Dunſter, in our route to Dulverton, we had a pleaſant ride for half a dozen miles, through a winding valley, and along the ſides of hills on the left, which came ſloping down with their woody ſkirts to the road. But we ſoon exchanged theſe vallies for a naked open country; and the woody hills for dreary ſlopes, cut into portions, by naked hedges, unadorned by a ſingle tree.

As we left Dulverton, in our way to Tiverton, we entered another pleaſing valley, wooded
thick

thick with oaks, which climbed a fteep on the right, and formed a hanging grove. On the left ran the Ex, a rapid rocky-channelled ftream, fhaded likewife with trees. Beyond the Ex, the ground rofe in a beautiful park-fcene ; in the midft of which ftands the houfe of Sir Thomas Acland.

From hence to Tiverton the country affords nothing that is ftriking. We had hills; but they were tame and uniform, following each other in fuch quick fucceffion, that we rarely found either a foreground or a diftance. As we mounted one, we had another immediately in view. At Tiverton are the remains of a caftle, which was formerly the manfion of the earls of Devonfhire.

SECT. XVII.

FROM hence we travelled through the same kind of hilly country towards Barnstaple. In our way we turned aside to see Lord Fortescue's at Castlehill, where we did not think we were sufficiently repaid for going so far out of our way. Lord Fortescue has improved a large tract of ground; but with no great taste or contrivance *. Into one error he has particularly fallen, that of over-building his improvements. From one stand we counted eight or nine buildings. This is the common error of improvers. It is a much easier matter to erect a temple, or a Palladian bridge, than to improve a piece of ground with simplicity and beauty, and give it the air of nature. One of his buildings, an old castle upon a hill, from which his place, I suppose, takes its name, stands beautifully. Little more, I should think, in the way of building, would have been ne-

---

* The reader will recollect this was written several years ago; and that many alterations may since have been made.

cessary.

ceffary. This lofty caftle might be object fufficient from almoft every part of his improvements.

As we approached Barnftaple, the view from
fome of the high grounds is very grand, compofed on one fide of Barnftaple-bay, and on
the other of an extenfive vale; the vale of
Taunton carrying the eye far and wide into its
rich and ample bofom. It is one of thofe
views which is too great a fubject for painting.
Art, confined by the rules of picturefque compofition, muft keep within the compafs of inch,
foot, and yard. But fuch flender confines
cannot roufe the imagination like thefe extenfive fcenes of nature. The painter, jealous of
his art, will fometimes deny this. If the picture, he tells us, be well painted, the fize is
nothing. His canvas (however diminutive)
has the effect of nature, and deceives the eye.
You are affected, fays he, by a landfcape feen
through the pane of a window. Why may you
not be equally affected by a landfcape *well
painted within the fame dimenfions ?*
   It is true, the eye is frequently impofed upon.
It is often *purpofely* mifled by *tricks* of deception.
                                                    But

But it is not under the idea of deception, that the *real* artift paints. He does not mean to *impofe* upon us, by making us believe that a picture of a foot long is an extended landfcape. All he wifhes is, to give fuch *characterijtic touches* to his picture, as may be able to roufe the imagination of the beholder. The picture is not fo much the *ultimate end*, as it is the *medium*, through which the ravifhing fcenes of nature are excited in the imagination.—We do indeed examine a picture likewife by the rules of picturefque compofition : but *this mode* of examination we are not now confidering. The rules of compofition ferve only to make the picture anfwer more effectually its *ultimate end*. We are now confidering only the effect which the picture produces on the mind of the fpectator, by carrying him forcibly, and yet willingly, with his *eyes open*, into thofe fcenes which it defcribes.

It is juft the fame in every fpecies of painting. The portrait-painter muft raife the idea of wit, or humour, or integrity, or good fenfe, or piety, or dignity, in the character of the perfon whofe portrait he reprefents, or he does nothing. In hiftory too, unlefs the picture roufe the imagination to fomething more than

you

you fee on the canvas, it leaves half its work undone. You coolly criticife it indeed by *pic-turefque rules*. But that is not all. It ought to raife in you thofe ideas and fentiments which paint cannot exprefs ; that is, it fhould produce fomething *in you*, which the painter could not produce *on his canvas*.

On the whole, then, the *true enjoyment of the picture* depends chiefly on the *imagination of the fpectator*; and as the utmoft the landfcape-painter can do, is to *excite the ideas* of thofe de-lightful fcenes which he reprefents, it follows, that *thofe fcenes themfelves* muft have a much greater effect on the imagination, than any *re-prefentation* of them which he can give; that is, the idea muft be much more ftrongly ex-cited by the *original*, than by a *reprefentative*. The fact is, art is a mere trifler compared with Nature. The efforts of both, it is true, may be called the works of God : but the difference lies here. In the efforts of *art*, God works with thofe little inftruments called *men* ; he works in miniature. But when he works in the grand ftyle of *nature*, the elements are his inftru-ments *.

---

* See the fubject of thefe laft pages treated in another view, in vol. ii. of For. Scen. p. 232.

S E C T. XVIII.

THE approach to Barnſtable from the lower grounds, is as beautiful as from the higher. The river, the bridge, the hills beyond it, and the eſtuary in the diſtance, make all together a good landſcape. The town itſelf alſo, ſituated about nine or ten miles from the ſea, ſtands in a pleaſant vale, ſhut in by hills, forming a ſemilunar cove around it. When the tides are high, it is almoſt inſulated. The flat grounds which lie immediately about it make an agreeable contraſt with the hills. Once theſe grounds were little better than marſhes; but by proper draining, they are now become beautiful meadows. In a word, Barnſtable is the pleaſanteſt town we met with in the weſt of Englaud.

From hence to Torrington the country is unintereſting; but between Torrington and Oakhampton it aſſumed a better appearance. In ſome parts of it we had grand diſtances; in other parts hanging woods; particularly a

very

very noble one belonging to Mr. Harris, which travelled with us a confiderable way on the left, and afforded us a view fometimes over it, and fometimes through it, but at all times pleafing.

From Oakhampton we vifited the falls of Lidford, which compofe the moft celebrated piece of fcenery in this country.

Lidford was formerly a town of the firft confequence in England. In William the Conqueror's time it was taxed pretty nearly on an equality with London. As tin was at that time the ftaple commodity of the country, Lidford might draw its confequence from being one of the principal marts of that metal. Here afterwards a ftannery-court was kept. The caftle, in which it was held, is ftill in being. It is a large fquare tower, rather out of repair, than in ruin. Near it ftands the parifh church; and at a diftance we had a view of another church, loftily feated, called Brentor. But the falls of Lidford are a mile and half from the caftle.

In ourway, we were to pafs a bridge, which, we were informed, was thrown over the rocky

fides

fides of two frightful precipices of the river Lid, each eighty feet high. The idea was terrific; and we expected a very grand fcene. But we were difappointed, from the omiffion of a fingle circumftance in the intelligence, which was, that the feparation between thefe two tremendous precipices is little more than the crevice of a rock; and, in fact, we had paffed it before we knew we had been upon it. It is only feen by looking over the battlements of the bridge. If the day be clear, you juft difcover the river foaming among rocks many fathoms below. If not, you muft be content with liftening to its roar. The mufic, however, is grand; for if the river be full, the notes fwell nobly from the bottom, varied, as they are, by afcending fo narrow and broken a funnel.

We were told a ftory of a London rider, who travelled this road in a ftormy night; and being defirous to efcape the rain, as quickly as he could, pufhed his horfe with what exertion his whip and fpurs could excite. The next morning he heard that Lidford bridge had been carried away in the night, when he recollected that his horfe had made a fingular bound in the middle of its courfe. In fact, he had feen bet-

ter

ter in the dark than his mafter, and had faved both his own life and his rider's by fpringing over the chafm.

In the back fettlements of Virginia, at the bottom of the Allegeny mountains, near a place called Stanton, there is a fpecimen of this mode of fcenery in a very grand ftyle. A valley winds feveral leagues in length, and yet is fcarce any where more than a hundred feet wide; though in many places it is two hundred and fifty deep. It is adorned in various parts with rock; and fecured by lofty mountains, covered with wood. This valley, through much of its courfe, is little more than the channel of a confiderable river. But in one part the rocks approximate fo nearly as to form a complete natural arch, not only over the river, but over the valley itfelf. When Nature *mimics* (if I may fo fpeak) the works of man, for bridges are not a natural production, you fee the comparative magnificence of her operations not only in their vaftnefs, but in the carelefs fimplicity with which they are wrought. When the hand of man throws an arch over a river or a chafm, he piles up a number of little ftones or bricks, fixing them with cement carefully and painfully, one upon

N 3   another,

another, in a certain regular fhape. All is
nicety, exactnefs, and precifion. If one ftone
be fixed awry, the whole ftructure is endan-
gered. But when Nature throws an arch, her
firft operation perhaps is, to bury deep in the
foil one end of fome vaft diagonal or horizontal ftratum of rock, flinging the other end
athwart over the chafm ; or, if that be not
fufficient, fhe unites it perhaps to the fragment
of a rock, formed in the fame manner on the
other fide of a valley. Sometimes fhe works
in a ftill grander ftyle, and forms her arch of
one fingle mafs of perforated ftone, which in
her way fhe hews into a vaft irregular furface.
In both operations it is evident a variety of
forms muft refult. Sometimes the arch is
pointed ; fometimes it is flat and horizontal ;
and often varied into fome namelefs form.
When the grand mafs of the edifice is thus
reared, Nature proceeds to ornament. She
leaves the cornice and the baluftrade to human
artifts. Her ornaments are of a different kind.
She firft fpreads the whole over with foil. In
the American arch here fpecified, the thicknefs
of the foil, including the fubftratum of rock, is
at leaft forty feet. This is a depth of foil fufficient for trees of confiderable fize ; many of
which

which adorn the arch. Among thefe Nature
has planted various fhrubs and hanging bufhes,
which are often highly coloured, and, ftreaming down, wave in the wind in great profufion.
Then perhaps with one of her broadeft pencils
fhe dafhes the fides of the rock with a thoufand beautiful ftains from moffes, and other in-
crufted vegetation of various kinds, which
finifh and complete the operation.

> Thus Nature works, as if to mock at Art,
> And in defiance of her rival powers.
> By thefe fortuitous and random ftrokes
> Performing fuch inimitable feats,
> As fhe with all her rules can never reach.

Such an arch is the American one we are
now furveying; which, on the authority of an
eye-witnefs, I have heard defcribed as a moft
magnificent ftructure of the kind. Sometimes,
I underftand, when the water is low, the traveller may walk under it, furvey its maffy
abutments, and looking up admire its tremendous roof, raifed at the vaft height of at leaft
two hundred feet above his head, and frofted
over with various knobs and rocky protube-
rances, which have ftood for ages, though they
continually threaten ruin. When he hath fatisfied his curiofity below, he may find a path,

N 4   which

which leads him to the top. There he meets a commodious road which is the only paſſage the inhabitants have over the valley. He finds alſo, in different parts, a rude rocky parapet; and if his curioſity carry him farther, he may cling to ſome well-rooted plant, and have a perpendicular view to the river below, as terrific as the view he had juſt had over his head. He will probably ſee alſo on one ſide, the river as it approaches, and on the other as it retires. Many beauties, I doubt not, might likewiſe be pointed out from this ſtation. But what I have heard chiefly noticed, are the rocky hills which environ the valley, and ſhoot into it, here and there, in vaſt promontories, covered with ſtately pines and oaks, which perhaps flouriſhed, as they now do, in the days of Columbus. Let us now return to humbler ſcenes.

The channel of the Lid, though contracted at the bridge, ſoon widens, both below it and above, and would afford many beautiful ſcenes to thoſe who had leiſure to explore them. This river riſes about three or four miles above Lidford, on the edge of Dartmore, and flowing through a barren plain, finds a ſmall rocky barrier, through which it has, in a courſe of ages, worn a whimſical paſſage. As it iſſues

from

from the check it meets with here, it falls about thirty feet into a fmall dell, which was not reprefented to us as a fcene of much beauty. But a little farther the banks rife on each fide; vegetation riots, the ftream defcends by a winding and rapid courfe; and the fkreens, though fmall, are often beautifully adorned with wood and rock. By this time the river approaches the bridge, where it is loft in the narrownefs of the channel, and, as I have juft obferved, becomes almoft fubterranean.

From the bridge we proceeded directly to what are emphatically called *the falls of Lidford*, which are about three miles below. We alighted at a farm-houfe, and were conducted on foot to the brow of a fteep woody hill, from which we had a grand view of Lidford-caftle, which appeared now, at a diftance, more proudly feated than it feemed to be when we rode paft it. Of the river we faw nothing, but could eafily make out its channel, under the abutments of grand promontories, which marked its courfe.

Having viewed this noble landfcape, we defcended the hill by a difficult winding path, and at the bottom found the Lid. The appearance which the river and its appendages made

here

here from the lower grounds were equally
pleafing, though not fo grand as from the
higher. Indeed no part of this magnificent
fcenery would be a difgrace to the wildeft and
moft picturefque country.

The *fall of the river*, which brought us hi-
ther, and which is the leaft confiderable part of
the fcenery, (for we had heard nothing of thefe
noble views,) is a mere garden-fcene. The
fteep woody hill, whofe fhaggy fides we had
defcended, forms at the bottom, in one of its
envelopes, a fort of little woody theatre; rather indeed too lofty when compared with its
breadth, if Nature had been as exact as Art
would have been, in obferving proportion.
Down the central part of it, which is lined
with fmooth rock, the river falls. This rocky
cheek is narrow at the top, but it widens as it
defcends, taking probably the form of the
ftream, when it is full. At the time we faw it,
it was rather a fpout than a cafcade; for though
it flides down a hundred and eighty feet, it
does not meet one obftruction in its whole
courfe, except a little check in the middle.
When the fprings are low, and the water has
not quantity enough to pufh itfelf forward in
one current, I have been told, it fometimes falls

3   in

in various little ftreams againft the irregulari-
ties of the rock, and is dafhed into a kind of
vapoury rain, which has a good effect.

This cafcade, it feems, is not formed by the
waters of the Lid, as we had fuppofed from its
name; but by a little ftream, which runs into
that river, rifing in the higher grounds, at the
diftance of about two miles from the cafcade.

SECT. XIX.

FROM Lidford we found a cheerful country to Taviſtock. In our way we paſſed
Brentor, which we had ſeen at a diſtance
when we firſt ſaw the caſtle of Lidford. It
is ſeated on the top of a mountain, and was
enveloped, when we rode paſt it, in all the
majeſty of darkneſs. In fact, it was ſo much
immerſed in clouds, that we could not even
diſtinguiſh its form ; and if we had not
ſeen it before at a diſtance, we ſhould have
been at a loſs to have known what it was;
though we ſhould certainly have thought it
rather a caſtle than a church. How very lofty
its ſituation is, may be ſuppoſed from its being
a good ſea-mark in opening Plymouth harbour,
though it ſtands at the diſtance of twenty miles
from the ſea.

At Taviſtock, from the appearance which
the river Tavey makes at the bridge, it is probable there may be ſome beautiful ſcenes along
its banks, but we had not time to explore
them.

As

As to the abbey, though it was once of mi-
tred dignity, and though a confiderable portion of it ftill remains, we did not obferve a
fingle paffage that was worth our notice. What
is left is worked up into barns, mills, and dwell-
ing-houfes. It may give the antiquarian pleafure to reverfe all this metamorphofis; to trace
back the ftable to the Abbott's lodge; the mill
to the refectory; and the malt-houfe to the
chapel: but the picturefque eye is fo far from
looking at thefe deeds of economy under the
idea of pleafure, that it paffes by them with
difdain, as heterogeneous abfurdities.

From Taviftock our next ftage was to Launcefton, through what feemed an unpleafant
country. But the whole road was involved
in fo thick a fog, that we faw but little of it.
Where we could have wifhed the fog to clear
up, it fortunately did, at a place called Axworthy. Here we defcended a fteep winding
woody hill, through the trees of which we had
beautiful views of tufted groves, and other objects on the oppofite fide. At the bottom we
found the Tamar, a fine ftream, adorned with
a picturefque bridge.

The

The road foon brought us to Launcefton, the capital of Cornwall, which is a handfome town. The caftle was formerly efteemed one of the ftrongeft fortreffes of the weft, as we may fuppofe at leaft from the name it bore, which was that of *Caftle-terrible*. During the civil wars of Charles I. it continued among the laft fupports of the royal caufe in thofe parts : though it has fuffered great dilapidations fince that time, its remains are ftill refpectable; and, what is more to the purpofe at prefent, they are picturefque. The great gate and road up to it, and the towers that adorn it, make a good picture. The ftately citadel makes a ftill better. It is raifed on a lofty eminence, and confifts of a round tower, encompaffed by the ruins of a circular wall; in which, through a wide breach, you difcover the internal ftructure to more advantage. The conftruction of this whole fortrefs is thought to have been very curious; and they who wifh to have a full account of it, may be gratified in Borlafe's Hiftory of Cornwall.

A little

A little to the north of Launceſton lies Wer-
rington, an eſtate belonging to the Duke of
Northumberland. The park contains many
beautiful ſcenes, conſiſting of hanging lawns
and woods, with a conſiderable ſtream, the
Aire, running through it. In ſome parts, where
the ground is high, the views are extenſive.
Many antiquarians ſuppoſe this to have been
the ſeat of Orgar Earl of Devonſhire, whoſe
beautiful daughter, Elfrida, is the ſubject of
one of the moſt affecting ſtories in the Engliſh
hiſtory, and one of the pureſt dramatic compoſitions in the Engliſh language.

Somewhere in this neighbourhood lived
Thomaſine Percival; at what time, I find not;
but the ſtory of this extraordinary woman is ſtill
current in the country. She was originally a
poor girl, and being beautiful, had the fortune
to marry a rich clothier, who dying early, left
her a well-jointured widow. A ſecond advantageous match, and a ſecond widowhood, in-
creaſed her jointure. Being yet in the bloom
of youth and beauty, her third huſband was
Sir John Percival, a wealthy merchant of London, of which he was Lord Mayor. He alſo
left

left her a widow with a large acceffion of fortune. Poffeffed of this accumulated property
fhe retired to her native country, where fhe
fpent her time and fortune altogether in works
of generofity and charity. She repaired roads,
built bridges, penfioned poor people, and por-
tioned poor girls, fetting an example, which
fhould never be forgotten among the extraordinary things of this country.

From Launcefton we travelled as far into
Cornwall as Bodmin, through a coarfe naked
country, and in all refpects as uninterefting as
can well be conceived. Of wood, in every
fhape, it was utterly deftitute.

Having heard that the country beyond Bodmin was exactly like what we had already paffed,
we refolved to travel no farther in Cornwall;
and inftead of vifiting the Land's-end, as we
had intended, we took the road to Lefcard,
propofing to vifit Plymouth in our return.

An antiquarian, it is probable, might find
more amufement in Cornwall than in almoft
any country in England. Even along the road
we

we faw ftones, and other objects, which feemed to bear marks both of curiofity and antiquity. Some of the ftones appear plainly to be monumental : the famous *Hurlers* we did not fee.

The naturalift alfo, the botanift, and the fof-filift, efpecially the laft, might equally find Cornwall a country full of interefting objects. Here his fearch would be rewarded by a great variety of metals, foffils, ftones, pebbles, and earths.

Here too the hiftorian might trace the various fcenes of Druid rites, and of Roman and Danifh power. Here alfo he might invefti-gate fome of the capital actions of the civil wars of the laft century ; and follow the foot-fteps of Fairfax, Sir Beville Grenville, Lord Hopton, and other great commanders in the weft. The battle of Stratton, in which the laft of thofe generals commanded, was an action mafterly enough to have added laurels to Cæfar, or the King of Pruffia. Indeed we could have wifhed to have gone a few miles farther to the north of this country, to have inveftigated the fcene of this action. Lord Clarendon has defcribed it fo accurately, that it can hardly be miftaken. It was a hill, fteep on all fides, bordering, if I underftand him rightly,

on

on a fandy common. On the top were encamped a body of 5400 of the parliament
forces, with thirteen pieces of cannon, under
the Earl of Stamford. At five o'clock in the
morning, on the 16th of May 1642, the roy-
alifts attacked them with very inferior force, in
four divifions, who mounted four different parts
of the hill at once. After a well-fought day,
they all met about three in the afternoon at the
top, and congratulated each other on having
cleared the hill of the enemy, and taken their
camp, baggage, ammunition, and cannon. The
fcene of fo notable an exploit may be ftill perhaps pointed out by the inhabitants of the
country. From Lord Clarendon's defcription,
however, it may certainly be found.

It is probable alfo that, in a picturefque
light, many of the caftles of this county might
have deferved attention; many of the coafts
might have amufed us with elegant fweeping
lines, and many of the bays might have been
nobly hung with rockey fcenery. We fhould
have wifhed alfo to have heard the winds howl
among the bleak promontories of the Land's-
end; to have feen, through a clear evening,
the light fall indiftinctly on the diftant ifles of
Scilly; and to have viewed the waves beating
round

round the rocks of that fingular fituation, Mount St. Michael. The lofs of this laft fcene we regretted more than any thing elfe. But to travel over defarts of drearinefs in queft of two or three objects feemed to be buying them at too high a price; efpecially as it is poffible they might have difappointed us in the end. Many a time has the credulous traveller gone in queft of fcenes on the information of others, and has found (fuch is the difference of opinions) that what gave his informant pleafure, has given him difguft.

SECT. XX.

IN returning from Bodmin, we paſſed over that part of Bradoc-downs, where Lord Hopton's prowefs was again ſhewn in giving a confiderable check to the parliament's forces in thofe parts. This wild heath, and much of the neighbouring country, is in the fame ſtyle of dreary landfcape, with that we had found between Launcefton and Bodmin. So very undifciplined the country ſtill is, that the wild ſtags of nature, in many parts, claim it as their own. We did not fee any of them; but we were told, they fometimes ſhew themfelves on the high moors about Bodmin and Lefcard.

And yet thefe are the lands, wild as they are, that are the richeſt of the country. They bear little corn, it is true; but it is very immaterial what the furface produces: the harveſt lies beneath. In this neighbourhood fome of the richeſt of the Cornifh mines are found; and Lefcard, where we now were, is one of the Coinage-towns, as they are called. Of thefe towns there are five, which are fcattered

about

about the different parts of Cornwall, where
mines are moſt frequent. After the tin is
pounded, and waſhed from the impurities
of the mine, it is melted, ſeparated from its
droſs, and run into large ſquare blocks, containing each about three hundred pounds
weight. In this form it is conveyed to the
Coinage-town, where it is aſſayed and ſtamped.
This ſtamp makes it a ſaleable commodity.

We had not, however, the curioſity to enter
any of theſe mines. Our buſineſs was only on
the ſurface. Great part of this country, it is
true, is in a ſtate of nature, which in general is
a ſtate of piⱥureſque beauty ; but here it was
otherwiſe. Our views not only wanted the
moſt neceſſary appendages of landſcape, wood,
and water, but even *form*. We might, perhaps,
have ſeen this part of Cornwall in an unfavourable light; as the ſweeping lines of a
country depend much for their beauty on the
light under which they are ſeen; but to us
they appeared heavy, unbroken, and unaccommodating. In the wild parts of Scotland,
where this drearineſs of landſcape often occurred, we had ſtill a diſtance to make amends
for the fore-grounds. It was rarely that we
had not a flowing line of blue mountains,

O 3   which

which gave a grandeur and dignity even to an
impoverifhed fcene. But in thefe wild parts
of Cornwall we fometimes faw a face of country, (which is rather uncommon in the wildeft
fcenes of nature,) without a fingle beauty to recommend it.

This drearinefs, however, had begun to improve before we arrived at Lefcard. Plantations, though meagre only, arofe in various
parts; and the country affumed fomewhat of a
more pleafing air; particularly on the right
towards Leftwithiel. The high grounds formed
interfections; fomething like a caftle appeared
on one of them, and the woody decorations of
landfcape in fome degree took place.

As we left Lefcard, the country ftill improved. Extenfive fides of hills, covered with
wood, arofe among the fore-grounds, and rang-
ing in noble fweeps, retired into diftance.
Thefe burfts of fylvan fcenery appeared with
particular beauty at a place called Brown's-
woods. Here too we were entertained with
an *incidental beauty*. The whole fky in front
was hung with dark clouds to the very fkirts
of the horizon. Behind us fhone the brighteft

ray

ray of an evening fun, not yet indeed fetting,
but very fplendid: and all this fplendor was
received by the tops of trees, which rofe directly in front, and being oppofed to the
gloomy tint behind them, made a moft bril-
liant appearance. This is among the moft
beautiful effects of an evening-fun. Thefe
effects are indeed as various as the forms of
landfcape which receive them; but nothing is
more *richly* enlightened than the tufted foliage
of a wood.

We now approached the fea, at leaft the
river Tamer, which is near its eftuary; and as
this coaft is perhaps one of the moft broken
and irregular of the whole ifland, we had feveral views of little creaks and bays, which
being furrounded with wood, are often beautiful. But they are beautiful at full-fea only;
at the ebb of the tide, each lake becomes an
oozy channel.

The picturefque beauty of a fcene of this
kind once coft a poor traveller dear. He had
long been in queft of a fituation for a houfe,
and found one at length offered to fale, exactly fuited to his tafte. It was a lake fcene;

in

in which a little peninfula, floping gently into the water, prefented from its eminence a pleaf-ing view of the whole. Charmed with what he had feen, he ruminated in his way home on the various improvements it might admit; and fearing a difappointment, entered, without farther fcrutiny, into an agreement with the owner, for a confiderable fum. But what was his aftonifhment, when, on taking poffeffion, his lake was gone, and in its room, a bed of filthy ooze! How did he accufe his rafhnefs, and blame his precipitate folly! In vain he wifhed to retract his bargain. In vain he pleaded, that he had been deceived; that he had bought a lake; and that, in fact, the ob-ject of his purchafe was gone. " You might " have examined it better," cried the unfeeling gentlemen of the law: " What have we to " do with your ideas of picturefque beauty? " We fold you an eftate, and if you impofed " upon yourfelf, you have nobody elfe to blame."

From the road, as we paffed, we had a view of Trematon-caftle, where a ftannery court is ftill kept, which had formerly very extenfive

privi-

privileges. *Trematon-law* is almoſt to this day an objeƈt of reverence among the common people of Cornwall.

Soon after, Saltaſh-bay opened on the left, and on the right, Hamoaz harbour, with many a gallant ſhip of war at anchor upon its ample boſom. Beyond the Hamoaz roſe the hanging lawns and woods of Mount Edgcomb, forming a noble back-ground to the ſcene.

At Saltaſh we had good views of the river Tamer, both above and below the town. A ſweeping bay is formed on each ſide, in many places at leaſt a mile in breadth. In both directions the banks are high, and the water retires beautifully behind jutting promontories.

Having croſſed the Tamer at Saltaſh, we had four miles farther to Plymouth. Through the whole way we had various views of the the ſound, Mount Edgcomb, Plymouth harbour, Hamoaz, Plymouth town, and Plymouth dock. From all theſe views together we were able to colleƈt a clear geographical idea of this celebrated harbour.

Two

Two rivers, the Tamer and the Plym, (the firſt of which is conſiderable,) meeting the ſea at the diſtance of about three miles aſunder, form at their ſeparate mouths two indented bays. Theſe two bays open into a third, which is the receptacle of both, and larger than either. The bay formed by the Tamer, is called the *Hamoaz*; that formed by the Plym is called *Plymouth Harbour*; and the large bay, into which they both open, is called the *Sound*. At the bottom of the Sound, where the two bays communicate with it, lies St. Nicolas, a large iſland, fortified with a caſtle and ſtrong works; which are intended to defend the entrance into both theſe inlets. The entrance into Hamoaz is very intricate; for the iſland can be paſſed only at that end next Plymouth; which makes the paſſage narrow and winding. The entrance at the other end is wide and direct; but is defended by a dangerous ſhelf of hidden rocks; the ſituation of which appears plainly at low-water from the ripling of the tide above them. The Corniſh ſide of Hamoaz is formed by Mount Edgcomb.

S E C T. XXI.

PLymouth-dock, or Dock-town, as it is often called, lies at the entrance of Hamoaz, and is about two miles diſtant from the town of Plymouth. It is chiefly worth viſiting, as it is the ſtation of the docks, ſtorehouſes, gun-wharfs, and other appendages of this noble arſenal; which is a wonderful ſight to thoſe who have ſeen nothing of the kind. The citadel too, and the victualling-office, which is cloſe to it; the bake-houſe alſo, and the ſlaughter-houſe, (whatever unpleaſant ideas may accompany the latter,) are all grand objects of their kind.

Among the things which attracted our attention at Plymouth-dock were the marble quarries. We ſaw ſeveral of the blocks poliſhed; and thought them more beautiful than any foreign marble. The ground is dark brown, the veining red and blue. The colours are ſoft in themſelves, and intermix agreeably;

whereas

whereas in the Sienna, and other foreign marbles, there is often, amidft all the richnefs of their colours, a glare and harfhnefs in their mixtures, difagreeable to the picturefque eye, which always wifhes to unite harmony with colouring. In the verde antique the tints are fufficiently foft; but they are fo much the fame, and broken into fuch minute parts, that they have no effect, when exhibited in quantity. After all, however, different kinds of marble are fuited to different purpofes. But I think there are two rules which fhould direct the choice of all marbles. In columns, and other large furfaces, the parts fhould be large; that is, the veins of the marble fhould be confpicuous. I think alfo that no marble, in any fituation, can be beautiful, unlefs there be a degree of foft-nefs and harmony in it: if it be veined, for in-ftance, the veins fhould, in fome parts, ftrike out boldly, and in other parts fink and retire, as it were, into the ground of the marble, leaving only flight traces of their colours here and there behind them. In both thefe refpects I have thought the columns in the hall at Kid-delfton in Derbyfhire models of beauty. It will, however, be underftood, that when *form*

or

or *infcription* is required, veined marble of any kind is improper. In fome works, as in moſt kinds of ornaments, the marble itſelf is the principal objeċt : in others, as in ſtatuary and inſcription, the marble is only the vehicle.

With the Plymouth marble, in its rough ſtate, moſt of the buildings of the dock are conſtruċted. The refuſe burns into excellent lime. Between Launceſton and Kellington, I have heard there is a ſpecies of marble found almoſt purely white ; but as I never heard of its being applied to any uſe, I ſuppoſe it is only of a ſpurious kind.

There is alſo another ſpecies of beautiful ſtone much in uſe at Plymouth, which is of Corniſh extraċtion, and is found chiefly on the moors, from whence it is called the *Moor-ſtone.* The beſt kind of it is a perfeċt granite, and will bear a poliſh ; though the ſpars ſometimes fly off in the operation, and leave an unequal ſurface. The more friable kind of this ſtone ſpangles the road with an excellent binding gravel.

Among the ſights of a dock-yard, the careening of a ſhip is not the leaſt piċtureſque. We happened to ſee an operation of this kind

in

in great perfection. The ship itself, lying on one fide, is a good object. Its great lines, which in an upright ftate are too regular, take now more pleafing forms; and while the rolling volumes of fmoke harmonize the whole, the fire glimmering, fparkling, or blazing, is fometimes enveloped in thefe black voluminous eddies, and fometimes brightening up, breaks through them in tranfient fpiry blazes.

But as *light* is beft fupported by *fhade*, a conflagration by *night*, from whatever caufe produced, has the grandeft effect. By day the effect depends chiefly on the fmoke, aided perhaps by fome accidental objects; as it was here by the pitchy fide of a veffel. But at night, the darknefs of the hemifphere makes the grandeft oppofition. The light is concentrated to one fpot, only varioufly broken, as it may happen to fall on different objects. At the fame time it receives the full beauty of gradation. The ruddy glow which fpreads far and wide into the regions of night, graduates, as it recedes from its centre, and becoming fainter and fainter, is at laft totally loft in the fhades of darknefs. A conflagration, therefore, by night prefents us with the jufteft

ideas

ideas of the great principles of light and fhade. It gives a *body of light varioufly broken*; and at length dying *gradually away*.

A common bonfire, furrounded by a few figures fcattered about it in groups, forms often a beautiful fcene. That paffage, in which Shakefpeare defcribes the camp-fires of the French and Englifh, gives us a different picture. In that defcription the fires are *diftant*; and the *paly flames* juft *umber* the faces that watch round them. Touched with the pencil, they fhould be marked only as ruddy fpecks: all diftinction of feature is loft. But round a *bonfire on the fpot* you fee action and paffion diftinctly reprefented; the hat waved, the agitated body, and the lips of the bawling mouth, all marked with the ftrongeft effects of light; while fome of the figures, which ftand between the eye and the fire, are as picturefquely diftinguifhed by being totally in fhade.

Grand indeed, though dreadful, is the conflagration of houfes; efpecially if thofe houfes have any dignity of form. The burfts of fire from windows and doors, the illumination of the internal parts of a ftructure, and the varied force of the fire on the different materials it meets with, which may be more or lefs com-
buftible,

buftible, are all circumftances highly picturefque. It may be added alfo, that wind makes a great difference in the appearance of a conflagration; and yet I know not whether its moft fplendid effects are not feen beft in a calm.

But the operations of war produce ftill grander effects of this kind. The burning of fhips is productive of greater ideas, and more picturefque circumftances, than the burning of houfes. The very reflections from the water add great beauty. But thefe reprefentations are among the difficult attempts of the pencil. Vanderveld, who did every thing well, and burnt many a fhip in a truly picturefque manner, failed moft in his grandeft work, the burning of the Armada. *Some parts* of his pictures on this fubject at Hampton Court are mafterly; but in *general* they are but an indif--ferent collection of Vanderveld's works. Probably the fubject was *impofed* on him; and when that is the cafe, the painter feldom arrives at the excellence which *his own fubjects* produce. It cannot well indeed be otherwife; for the *choice of a fubject* is, in other words, *that juft arrangement* of it, which he conceives in his own mind, both in regard to compo-

fition

fition and light. So that when a fubject is
impofed, the arrangement is to *feek* ; and it is
probable, he may not eafily find one that fuits
his fubject. Befides, he fets to it without that
enthufiafm which fhould animate his pencil.
When the Emprefs of Ruffia, therefore, employed Sir Jofhua Reynolds, fhe did well in
leaving him to choofe his own fubject. One
thing, indeed, which injures Vanderveld in
burning the Armada picturefquely, is the number of fires he is obliged to introduce, which
can never have fo good an effect as one.

But among all the grand exhibitions of this
kind, the fiege of Gibraltar furnifhes two of
the nobleft. They had every circumftance to
recommend them. They were grand in their
own nature ; they were connected with great
and profperous events, which is a recommendation of any fubject; and they were actions
performed in the night. The firft relates to
the burning of the enemy's batteries by a fally
from the garrifon ; the fecond, to the deftruc-
tion of the battering fhips. I fhall give them
both in the words of a publifhed Journal of
that fiege, in which the effects are well defcribed *.

* See Drinkwater's Account of the Siege of Gibraltar, p. 201.

P   " Nov.

" Nov. 27, 1781. The batteries were foon
" in a ftate for the fire-faggots to operate, and
" the flames fpread with aftonifhing rapidity
" into every part. The column of fire and
" fmoke, which rolled from the works, beauti-
" fully illumined the troops, and neighbour-
" ing objects ; forming all together a *coup*
" *d'œil* not poffible to be defcribed."

" Sept. 13, 1782. About an hour after mid-
" night one of the battering-fhips was com-
" pletely in flames ; and by two o'clock fhe
" appeared one continued blaze from ftem to
" ftern. Between three and four o'clock, fix
" other fhips were on fire. The light thrown
" out on all fides by the flames, illumined the
" rock, and all the neighbouring objects ;
" forming, with the conftant flafhes of our
" cannon, a mingled fcene of fublimity and
" terror *." The former of thefe fcenes would
have made a good picture : the latter, if reprefented, fhould be taken, when one fhip only
was completely in flames, with fmall appearances of fire in fome of the others.

At the end of the 8th book of Homer we
have the effects of an illumination very pictu-

* See Drinkwater's Account of the Siege, p. 287.

refquely

refquely detailed. Hector aving driven the Greeks to their intrenchments, was prevented by the night from completing his victory. Refolving therefore to pufh it the next morning, inftead of retreating to Troy, he encamped under its walls in the field of battle, where

> Unnumbered flames before proud Ilion blaze,
> And lighten glimmering Xanthus with their rays.
> The long reflections of the diftant fires
> Gleam on the walls, and tremble on the fpires.
> A thoufand piles the dufky horrors gild,
> And fhoot a fhadowy luftre o'er the field.
> Full fifty guards each flaming pile attend,
> Whofe umber'd arms, by fits, thick flafhes fend.

Homer, however, has nothing to do with moft of thefe picturefque images. They are only to be found in Pope's tranflation. Though it may be fafhionable to depreciate this work, as a tranflation, it muft at leaft be owned, that Pope, who was a painter, has enriched his original with many of the ideas of his art.

But ftill, in all thefe operations, however grand, the fire ravages only the *works of man*. To fee a conflagration in perfection, we muft fee the *elements engaged*. Nothing is *eminently grand*, but the exertion of an *element*. The effect of the *air* is grand, when excited by a ftorm. Piles of *earth* or *mountains* are fuperbly grand.

grand. The *ocean* in a storm is still grander: and the effect of *fire*, when let loose in its full fury, carries the idea of grandeur to a still greater height.

One of the most astonishing effects of this kind, which is any where to be met with, may be found in the 70th volume of the Philosophical Transactions, in a letter from Sir William Hamilton. It contains the account of an eruption of Mount Vesuvius, in the autumn of the year 1779. The whole relation is full of grand ideas; but the parts of it, to which I particularly allude, were the *concluding efforts* of the eruption; from which I shall select a few circumstances.

The relater, who was an eye-witness, tells us, that on Saturday the 7th of August, as he was watching the agitations of the mountain from the mole of Naples, which gave him a distinct view of it, a violent storm came on, just as the volcano was throwing out some of its fiercest fires. The clouds of black smoke sometimes covered great part of the fire; at other times disparting, presented it in fuller view. This awful conjunction of light and shadow, was farther assisted by various tints, which were produced by lights reverberated
from

from the clouds, and by pale flashes of light-
ning, which were continually issuing from
them.

But the appearance of the volcano, the
next day, was still more sublime. About nine
o'clock in the morning, a loud report issued from
the mountain, which shook the houses of Por-
tici to such a degree, as to alarm the inhabitants for their safety, and drive them into the
streets. Immediately volumes of liquid fire,
or rather, as the relater describes it, fountains
of red-hot lava, shot upwards to such an amaz-
ing height, that they seemed three times as
high as the mountain itself, which is computed
to rise three thousand feet from the level of the
sea. Together with these volumes of liquid
fire, vast clouds of the blackest smoke succeeded
each other in bursts, intercepting this splendid
brightness here and there by masses of the
darkest hue.

The wind was south-west; and though gentle, was sufficient to put the smoke into motion, removing it by degrees so as to form behind the fire a vast curtain, stretching over
great part of the hemisphere. To add to the
solemnity, this black curtain was continually
disparted by pale, momentary, electric fires.

In

In the mean time, the other parts of the ſky were clear, and the ſtars ſhone bright. The contraſt was glorious beyond imagination. The ſplendor, which was ſufficiently balanced by the ſhadowy curtain behind it, illumined the ſea, which was perfectly calm, far and wide, and added much to the ſublimity of the ſcene.

Some of the fiery lava being thrown on mount Somna, in the neighbourhood of Veſuvius, its woods were frequently in a blaze. This introduced a ſecondary light, very different in its tint, either from the fiery red of the volcano, or the ſilvery blue of the electric fire.

This grand and awful viſion, in which as ſublime *an effect of light and ſhade* was preſented, as Nature perhaps ever exhibited before, laſted about half an hour.

I make no apology for introducing all theſe grand effects of fire, as I never think myſelf out of ſight of my ſubject, when I can lay hold of any pictureſque idea.

S E C T. XXII.

OUR curiosity having been gratified among
the dock-yards at Plymouth, led us next
to visit Mount Edgcomb.

The promontory of Mount Edgcomb running a considerable way into the sea, forms, as
was just observed, one of the cheeks of the entrance of Hamoaz-harbour, which is here half
a mile across. The whole promontory is four
or five miles long, and three broad. In shape
it is a perfect *dorsum*, high in the middle, and
sloping gradually on both sides towards the
sea; in some places it is rocky and abrupt.

Lord Edgcomb's house stands half way up
the ascent, on the Plymouth side, in the midst
of a park, containing an intermixture of wood
and lawn. It makes a handsome appearance
with a tower at each corner; but pretends
only to be a comfortable dwelling.

The great object of Mount Edgcomb is
the grandeur of the views. As we advanced
towards the summit of the promontory, we
saw, in various exhibitions, on one side, all the

intri-

intricacies and creeks, which form the harbour of Plymouth; with an extenfive country fpreading beyond it into very remote diftance; and fcattered with a variety of objects; among which we diftinguifhed the well-known features of Brentor.

The other fide of the promontory overlooks the Sound, which is the great rendezvous of the fleets fitted out at Plymouth; though feamen fpeak very indifferently of its anchorage. One of the boundaries of this extenfive bay is a reach of land running out into pointed rocks; the other is a lofty fmooth promontory, called the Ram's-head. The top of this promontory is adorned with a tower, from which notice is given at Plymouth, by a variety of fignals, of the number of fhips, and their quality, that appear in the offing.

Between the Ram's-head and Mount Edgcomb is formed a fmaller inlet, called Caufandbay, at the head of which lies Kingfton. Before this little town rode a large fleet of what appeared to be fifhing boats; but we were informed that moft of them were fmuggling veffels.

The fimplicity of the few objects which form the Sound on one fide, made a pleafing contraft

contraft with the intricacies of the Plymouth-
coaft on the other.

At the diftance of about three leagues from
the Ram's-head, ftands the Edyftone light-
houfe. We could juft difcern it, as it caught a
gleam of light, like a diftant fail.

Having viewed from the higher grounds
of Mount Edgcomb this immenfe landfcape,
which is, on both fides, a mere map of the
country, and has little *picturefque beauty*, efpecially on the Plymouth fide, we defcended the
promontory, and were carried on a lower ftage
round its utmoft limits.

The grounds here are profufely planted. On
that fide which overlooks Caufand-bay, the
plantations are only young; but on the other,
which confifts of at leaft half the promontory,
they are well-grown, and form the moft pleafing fcenes about Mount Edgcomb. That immenfe map, as it lay before the eye *in one view*
from the higher grounds, and appeared varioufly broken and fcattered, was now divided
into portions, and fet off by good foregrounds.
Some of thefe views are pleafing; but in general they are not picturefque. A large piece
of water full of moving objects, makes a part
of

of them all ; and this will always prefent at least an amufing fcene.

The trees, both evergreens and deciduous, are wonderfully fine, confidering their fea-afpect. But chiefly the pine-race feems to thrive; and among thefe the pinafter, which, one fhould imagine, from its hardy appearance, to be indigenous to the foil. The woodman would diflike that great abundance of hoary mofs, which bedecks both it and moft of the other plants of this marine fcenery ; but to the picturefque eye, the vegetation feems perfect ; and the mofs a beauty. It is mofs of a peculiar form, at leaft of an unufual growth. Its hue is generally cerulean, with a ftrong touch here and there of Naples-yellow, mixed with other pleafing tints, which being fcattered profufely about the whole plantation, give it an uncommon richnefs. In thefe woods the arbutus grows in great perfection, and many other fhrubs, which are generally found only in fheltered fituations.

Befides a luxuriance of wood, a variety of rocky fcenery embellifhed our walk, efpecially about the vertical point of the promontory. It is a well-coloured brown rock ; which appears

in

in all forms. Nor is it bald and naked, but every where garniſhed with twiſting boles and hanging ſhrubs.

Upon the whole, though there are many formalities about Mount Edgcomb, terraces particularly, and viſtas near the houſe, a few puerilities alſo *, and too little advantage taken every where of the circumſtances which nature has pointed out ; yet it is certainly a noble ſituation, and very well worth the attention of a traveller.

---

* The reader will recollect when this was written.

S E C T. XXIII.

AMONG the curiofities of this coaft, the Edyftone light-houfe is not one of the leaft. About three leagues beyond Plymouth-found, in a line nearly between Start-point and the Lizard, lie a number of low rocks, exceedingly dangerous at all times, but efpecially when the tides are high, which render them invifible. On thefe rocks it had long been thought neceffary to place fome monitory fignal. But the difficulty of conftructing a light-houfe was great. One of the rocks indeed, which compofe this reef, is confiderably larger than the reft: yet its dimenfions are ftill narrow; it is often covered with water, and frequently, even in the calmeft weather, furrounded by a fwelling fea, which makes it difficult to land upon it; and much more fo to carry on any work of time and labour. The uncommon tumult of the fea in this place is occafioned by a peculiarity in the rocks. As they all flope and point to the north-eaft, they fpread their inclined fides, of courfe, to the fwelling tides and ftorms

2   of

of the Atlantic. And as they continue in this
shelving direction many fathoms below the surface of the sea, they occasion that violent work-
ing of the water, which the seamen call a *ground
swell*. So that after a storm, when the surface of
the sea around is perfectly smooth, the swells
and agitation about these rocks are dangerous.
From these continual eddies the Edystone derives its name.

The first light-house of any consequence,
erected on this rock, was undertaken by a person of the name of Winstanley, in the reign of
King William. Mr. Winstanley does not appear to have been a man of solidity and judgment sufficient to erect an edifice of this kind.
He had never been noted for any capital work;
but much celebrated for a variety of trifling and
ridiculous contrivances. If you set your foot
on a certain board in one of his rooms, a
ghost would start up; or if you sat down in an
elbow-chair, its arms would clasp around you.
His light-house, which was built of wood, par-
took of his whimsical genius. It was finished
with galleries, and other ornaments, which en-
cumbered it, without being of any use. It
was, however, on the whole, much admired as
a very ingenious edifice, and Winstanley certainly

tainly deferved the credit of being the firft pro-
jector of a very difficult work. He had fixed
it to the rock by twelve maffy bars of iron,
which were let down deep into the body of the
ftone. It was generally indeed thought well
founded; and the architect himfelf was fo con-
vinced of its ftability, that he would often fay,
he wifhed for nothing more than to be fhut
up in it during a violent ftorm. He at length
had his wifh; for he happened to be in it, at
the time of that memorable ftorm on the 26th
of November 1703, which hath been already
mentioned *. As the violence, however, of the
tempeft came on, the terrified architect began
to doubt the firmnefs of his work: it trembled
in the blaft, and fhook in every joint. In vain
he made what fignals of diftrefs he could in-
vent, to bring a boat from the fhore. The terrors of the ftorm were fuch, that the boldeft
veffel durft not face it. How long he continued in this melancholy diftrefs is unknown;
but in the morning no appearance of the light-
houfe was left. It and all its contents, during
that terrible night, were fwept into the fea.
This cataftrophe furnifhed Mr. Gay with the

* See pages 156 and 168.

follow-

following fimile in his Trivia, which was written a few years after the event :

> So when fam'd Edyfton's far-fhooting ray,
> That led the failor through the ftormy way,
> Was from its rocky roots by billows torn,
> And the high turret in the whirlwind born,
> Fleets bulged their fides againft the craggy land,
> And pitchy ruins blacken'd all the ftrand.

A light-houfe was again conftructed on this
rock before the conclufion of Queen Anne's
reign. It was undertaken by one Rudyard,
who built it alfo of wood, but having feen
his predeceffor's errors, avoided them. He
followed Winftanley's idea in the mode of fixing his ftructure to the rock ; but he chofe a
plain circular form, without any gallery, or
ufelefs projecting parts for the ftorm to faften
on. To give ftability alfo to his work, he judicioufly introduced, as ballaft at the bottom,
270 tons of ftone. In fhort, every precaution
was taken to fecure it againft the fury of the
two elements of wind and water, which had deftroyed the laft. But it fell by a third. Late
one night, in the year 1755, it was obferved
from the fhore to be on fire. Its upper works
having been conftructed of light timber, probably could not bear the heat. It happened
fortunately that Admiral Weft rode with a

fleet

fleet at that time in the Sound; and being fo
near the fpot, he immediately manned two or
three fwift boats. Other boats put off from
the fhore; but though it was not ftormy, it
was impoffible to land. In the mean time the
fire having defcended to the lower parts of
the building, had driven the poor inhabitants
upon the fkirts of the rock; where they were
fitting difconfolate, when affiftance arrived.
They had the mortification, however, to find
that the boats, through fear of being dafhed in
pieces, were obliged to keep aloof. At length
it was contrived to throw coils of rope upon
the rock, which the men tied round them,
and were dragged on board through the
fea. The cafe of one of thefe poor fellows,
who was above 90 years of age, was fingular.
As he had been endeavouring to extinguifh the
fire in the cupola, where it firft raged, and was
looking up, the melted lead from the roof came
trickling down upon his face and fhoulders.
At Plymouth he was put into a furgeon's
hands; and, though much hurt, he appeared
to be in no danger. He conftantly, however,
affirmed, that fome of the melted lead had fallen
down his throat. This was not believed, as it
was thought he could not have furvived fuch a
circum-

circumſtance. In twelve days he died; and
Mr. Smeaton ſays, he ſaw the lead, after it had
been taken out of his ſtomach; and that it
weighed ſeven ounces *.

The next light-houſe, which is the preſent
one, was built by Mr. Smeaton, and is conſtructed on a plan, which it is hoped will ſe-
cure it againſt every danger. It is built entirely
of ſtone, in a circular form. Its foundations
are let into a ſocket in the rock, on which it
ſtands, and of which it almoſt makes a part;
for the ſtones are all united with the rock, and
with each other, by maſſy dove-tails. The cement uſed in this curious maſonry is the lime
of Watchet †, from whence Mr. Smeaton contrived to bring it barrelled up in cyder-caſks;
for the proprietors will not ſuffer it to be ex-
ported in its crude ſtate. The door of this ingenious piece of architecture is only the ſize of
a ſhip's gun-port; and the windows are mere
loop-holes, denying light to exclude wind.
When the tide ſwells above the foundation of
the building, the light houſe makes the odd appearance of a ſtructure emerging from the
waves. But ſometimes a wave riſes above the

* See Mr. Smeaton's Account of the Edyſtone.
† See page 169.

Q   very

very top of it, and circling round, the whole looks like a column of water, till it breaks into foam, and fubfides.

The care of this important beacon is committed to four men; two of whom take the charge of it by turns, and are relieved every fix weeks. But as it often happens, efpecially in ftormy weather, that boats cannot touch at the Edyftone for many months, a proper quantity of falt provifion is always laid up, as in a fhip victualled for a long voyage. In high winds fuch a briny atmofphere furrounds this gloomy folitude from the dafhing of the waves, that a man expofed to it could not draw his breath. At thefe dreadful intervals the two forlorn inhabitants keep clofe quarters, and are obliged to live in darknefs and ftench; liftening to the howling ftorm, excluded in every emergency from the leaft hope of affiftance, and without any earthly comfort, but what is adminiftered from their confidence in the ftrength of the building in which they are immured. Once, on relieving this forlorn guard, one of the men was found dead, his companion chufing rather to fhut himfelf up with a putrifying carcafe, than, by throwing it into the fea, to incur the fufpicion of murder. In

fine

fine weather, thefe wretched beings juft fcram-
ble a little about the edge of the rock, when the
tide ebbs, and amufe themfelves with fifhing;
which is the only employment they have, except that of trimming their nightly fires.

Such total inaction and entire feclufion from
all the joys and aids of fociety, can only be
endured by great religious philofophy, which
we cannot imagine they feel ; or by great ftu-
pidity, which in pity we muft fuppofe they
poffefs.

Yet though this wretched community is fo
fmall, we were affured it is generally a fcene of
mifanthropy. Inftead of fuffering the recollection of thofe diftreffes and dangers in which
each is deferted by all but one, to endear that
one to him, we were informed the humours
of each were fo foured, that they preyed both
on themfelves, and on each other. If one fat
above, the other was commonly found below.
Their meals too were folitary, each, like a
brute, growling over his food alone.

We are forry to acknowledge a picture like
this to be a likenefs of human nature. In fome
gentle minds we fee the kind affections *rejoice*
in being beckoned even from fcenes of inno-

cence,

cence, mirth, and gaiety, to mingle the sympa-
thetic tear with affliction and diftrefs. But experience fhews us, that the heart of man is
equally fufceptible of the malevolent affections;
and religion joins in confirming the melancholy truth. The *picturefque eye*, in the mean-
time, furveys natural and moral evil, under
characters entirely different. Darken the ftorm;
let loofe the winds; let the waves overwhelm
all that is fair and good; the ftorm will be fublime, and the cataftrophe pathetic; while the
moral tempeft is dreary, without grandeur, and
the cataftrophe afflicting, without one picturefque idea.

The emolument of this arduous poft is
twenty pounds a year, and provifions while on
duty. The houfe to live in may be fairly
thrown into the bargain. The whole together
is, perhaps, one of the leaft eligible pieces of
preferment in Britain: and yet from a ftory,
which Mr. Smeaton relates, it appears there
are ftations ftill more ineligible. A fellow, who
got a good livelihood by making leathern-pipes
for engines, grew tired of fitting conftantly at
work, and folicited a light-houfe man's place,
which, as competitors are not numerous, he
obtained.

obtained. As the Edyſtone-boat was carrying him to take poſſeſſion of his new habitation, one of the boatmen aſked him, what could tempt him to give up a profitable buſineſs to be ſhut up, for months together, in a pillar ? " Why," ſaid the man, " becauſe I did not like con- " finement."

S E C T. XXIV.

AT Plymouth we heard much of the scenery upon the Tamer, of which we had had a little specimen at Axworthy *. We resolved therefore to navigate that river as far as the Weir, which is about twenty-two miles above Plymouth, and as far as we could have the advantage of the tide. Procuring therefore a good boat, and four stout hands from the Ocean man of war, then lying in the Hamoaz, we set sail with a flowing tide.

The river Tamer rises from the mountains of Hartland, near Barnstaple-bay, in the north of Devonshire, and, taking its course almost due south, divides that county from Cornwall. No river can be a more complete boundary. As it approaches Plymouth, it becomes a noble estuary. The Hamoaz is esteemed, after Portsmouth, the best station for ships of war upon the British coast. This grand bay, which was the first scene we investigated on the Tamer, is

* See page 189.

about

about a mile in breadth, and feven miles in length ; though the larger fhips we obferved feldom to anchor above a league from the fea. Its banks on each fide, though rather low, are by no means flat. They are generally culti-vated ; and the fhore is finifhed by a narrow edging of rock.

The next view we had of any confequence, was the opening towards St. German's on the left. This is a creek about three leagues in length. The woods of Anthony occupy one fide of the opening; and a houfe which appeared at a diftance in the centre, is Ince, a feat of the Killigrews.

Soon after, we came in fight of Saltafh, which ftands high, but affords no very pic-turefque appearance. When we croffed the ferry the day before, the views of the creek from the hill prefented a beautiful fcene, both above and below the town*; but when the eye is ftationed *upon* the water, the retiring reaches of the river are loft, and the landfcape is much impaired.

Our next fcene was the opening of the Tavey into the Tamer. Sir Harry Trelaw-

* See page 201.

Q 4

ney's

ney's houfe was one of the principal objects of this view. The diftance was compofed chiefly of the Dartmore hills. The banks of the Tamer were ftill low, and cultivated; and bore no proportion to the extent of the water, which did not begin to contract itfelf, nor the banks to fwell, till we had proceeded nine or ten miles up the river.

The firft fcene, which in any degree engaged our attention, was compofed of the woods of Pentilly, on the Cornifh fide. The houfe too is a good object, and a building at the bottom of the bank has a picturefque appearance; though its dignity was degraded when we learned it was only a lime-kiln. Lime is the chief commodity of trade on this river, employing many large boats in tranfporting it; and the lime-kilns, which we fee in many places on its banks, are of fuch noble dimenfions, that they may, at a little diftance, be miftaken for caftles, without any imputation on the underftanding. They are among the greateft ornaments of the river. The background of the fcenery of Pentilly, is a lofty bank adorned with a tower, to which belongs a hiftory.

Mr.

Mr. Tilly, once the owner of Pentilly-houfe, was a celebrated atheift of the laft age. He was a man of wit, and had by rote all the ribaldry and common-place jefts againft religion and fcripture; which are well fuited to difplay pertnefs and folly, and to unfettle a giddy mind, but are offenfive to men of fenfe, whatever their opinions may be, and are neither intended nor adapted to inveftigate truth. The brilliancy of Mr. Tilly's wit, however, carried him a degree farther than we often meet with in the annals of prophanenefs. In general the witty atheift is fatisfied with entertaining his *contemporaries*; but Mr. Tilly wifhed to have his fprightlinefs known to *pofterity*. With this view, in ridicule of the refurrection, he obliged his executors to place his dead body, in his ufual garb, and in his elbow-chair, upon the top of a hill, and to arrange, on a table before him, bottles, glaffes, pipes, and tobacco. In this fituation he ordered himfelf to be immured in a tower of fuch dimenfions, as he prefcribed; where he propofed, he faid, patiently to wait the event. All this was done, and the tower, ftill inclofing its tenant, remains as a monument of his impiety and prophanenefs.

nefs. The country people fhudder as they go near it :

> —— Religio pavidos terrebat agreftes
> Dira loci :—fylvam, faxumque tremebant.

As we failed farther up the river, we came in view of the rocks and woods of Coteil, which are ftill on the Cornifh fide, and afford fome beautiful fcenery. Here we had grand fweeping hills, covered with wood. At the bottom of one of them ftands a noble lime-kiln-caftle, which is relieved by a lofty background.

Near the bottom of another ftands a fmall Gothic ruin, fituated, with much picturefque beauty, in a woody recefs. It was formerly a votive chapel, built by a chief of the Coteil family; though fome fay by one of the Edgcombs. Its founder had engaged on the unfuccefsful fide, during one of the periods of the dubious wars of York and Lancafter. His party being beaten, he fled for his life ; and as he was a man of confequence, was clofely purfued. The Tamer oppofed his flight. He made a fhort vow to the Virgin Mary, threw himfelf into the river, and fwam fafe to the promontory, before which we now lay on our

oars,

oars. His upper garment, which he had thrown off, floated down the ftream; and giving occafion to believe he had perifhed, checked the ardour of purfuit. In the mean time Coteil lurked in his own woods, till a happier moment; and in the day of fecurity raifed this chapel to the holy Virgin, his protectrefs, who had the full honour of his efcape.

We have the ftory fometimes told otherwife, and given to the times of Charles I.; but a ftory of fo late a date, one fhould imagine, might have been better afcertained, than this feems to be; and if the chapel have any connection with the ftory, it is much more credible, that a votive-chapel fhould have been erected in the 15th century, when we know they were common, than in the 17th, when fuch ftructures were never heard of.

At Coteil-houfe we landed, which is entirely furrounded with wood, and fhut out from the river. If it were a little opened, it might both fee and be feen to advantage. To the river particularly it would prefent a good object; as it ftands on a bold knoll, and is built in the form of a caftle. But it is a deferted manfion, and occupied only as a farm-houfe. Here we refrefhed ourfelves with tea, and larded our bread,

after

after the fashion of the country, with clouted cream.

Round this old mansion grew some noble trees; and among them the Spanish chesnut, full grown, and spread out in huge massy limbs. We thought these chesnuts scarce inferior in grandeur to the proudest oaks. The chesnut, on which Salvator Rosa has hung Edipus, is exactly one of them.

We had now sailed a considerable way up the Tamer, and, during the whole voyage, had been almost solely obliged to the Cornish shores for amusement. But the Devonshire coast, as if only collecting its strength, burst out upon us at Calstock, in a grander display of lofty banks, adorned with wood and rock, than any we had yet seen, and continued without interruption through the space of a league.

But it is impossible to describe scenes, which, though *strongly marked*, have no *peculiar* features. In Nature these lofty banks are infinitely varied. The face of each rock is different; it projects differently: it is naked, or it is adorned ; or, if adorned, its ornaments are of different kinds. In short, Nature's variations are as infinite on the face of a rock, as in the

face

face of a man. Each requires a diftinct portrait to characterize it juftly; while language
can no more give you a full idea of one, than
it can of the other.

With the views of Calftock we finifhed our
voyage up the Tamer; and though the banks of
the river were diverfified both with rocks and
woods, with open and contracted country; yet,
confidering the fpace through which we had
failed, and the high commendations we had
heard of this river, it was, on the whole, lefs
a fcene of amufement, than we had expected
to find it. We had a few grand views; but
in general the navigators of the Tamer find
only fome of the common characteriftics of a
river :

   ——Longos fuperant flexus, variifque teguntur
Arboribus; viridefque fecant placido æquore fylvas.

All is beautiful, fylvan, and highly pleafing; but
if you afk what we faw, we can only fay *in ge-*
neral, that we faw rocks, trees, groves, and
woods. In fhort, the whole is amufing, but
not picturefque; it is not fufficiently divided
into portions adapted to the pencil.

The fcenery itfelf, on the banks of the Tamer, is certainly good; but had it even been
better, the form of the river could not have

                         fhewn

shewn it to much picturesque advantage. The reaches are commonly too long, and admit little winding. We rarely trace the course of the river by the perspective of one skreen behind another; which in river views is often a beautiful circumstance: and yet, if one of the banks be lofty, broken into large parts, and falling away in good perspective, the length of the reach may possibly be an advantage. In some parts of the Tamer we had this grand lengthened view; but in other parts we wished to have had its continued reaches more contracted.

These remarks, however, it must be observed, affect a river only in *navigating* it. When we are thus on a *level* with its surface, we have rarely more than a fore-ground; at most we have only a first distance. But when we take a higher stand, and view a remote river, lofty banks become then an incumbrance; and instead of discovering, they hide its winding course. When the distance becomes still more remote, the valley through which the river winds should be open, and the country flat, to produce the most pleasing effect.

In the immense rivers that traverse continents, these ideas are all lost. As you sail up

such

such a vaſt ſurface of water, as the Miſſiſſippi, for inſtance, the firſt ſtriking obſervation is, that perſpective views are entirely out of the queſtion. If you wiſh to examine either of its ſhores, you muſt deſert the main channel; and, knowing that you are in a river, make to one ſide or the other.

As you approach within half a league of one of the ſides, you will perhaps ſee ſtretches of ſand-banks, or iſlands covered with wood, extending along the ſhore, beyond the reach of the eye, which have been formed by de-predations made on the coaſt by the river; for when the winds rage, this vaſt ſurface of water is agitated like a ſea; and has the ſame power over its ſhores. As the trees of theſe regions are in as grand a ſtyle as the rivers themſelves, you ſometimes ſee vaſt excavations, where the water has undermined the banks, in which im-menſe roots are laid bare, and, being waſhed clean from the ſoil, appear twiſted into various forms, like the gates of a cathedral.

Though the banks of the Miſſiſſippi, we are told, are generally flat, you frequently ſee beau-tiful ſcenery upon them. Among the vaſt woods which adorn them, are many groves of cypreſſes; to which a creeping plant, called

the

the Liane, is often attached. What kind of flower it bears, I have not heard; but if it be not too profuse, it muft be very ornamental: hanging from tree to tree, and connecting a whole cyprefs-grove together with rich feftoons.

Thefe woods are interfperfed alfo with lawns, where you fee the wild deer of the country feeding in herds. As they efpy the veffel gliding paft, they all raife their heads at once, and ftanding a moment, with pricked ears, in amazement, they turn fuddenly round, and darting acrofs the plain, hide themfelves in the woods.

From fcenes of this kind, as you coaft the river, you come perhaps to low marfhy grounds; where fwamps, overgrown with reeds and rufhes, but of enormous growth, extend through endlefs tracts, which a day's failing cannot leave behind. In thefe marfhes the alligator is often feen bafking near the edge of the river, into which he inftantly plunges on the leaft alarm; or perhaps you defcry his hideous form creeping along the fedges, fometimes hid, and fometimes difcovered, as he moves through a clofer, or more open path.

Contrafts, like thefe, between the Tamer and the Miffiffippi, are amufing, and fet each fcene

off

off to more advantage. The Tamer may be called a noble river; but what is it in point of grandeur, when compared with the Miſſiſſippi, which, at the diſtance of two thouſand miles from the ſea, is a wider ſtream than the Tamer, where it falls into it? On the other hand, though the Miſſiſſippi, no doubt, has its beauty; yet as a river, it loſes as much in this reſpect, when compared with the Tamer, as it gained in point of grandeur. In the Miſſiſſippi you ſeek in vain for the rocky banks and winding ſhores which adorn the Tamer, and are the glory of river-ſcenery.

To theſe contraſts I ſhall juſt add one more. As Lord Macartney and his ſuit, in their way to Canton, ſailed down one of the rivers of China, they paſſed under a rock of grey mar-ble, which aroſe from the water to the amaz-ing perpendicular height of ſix hundred feet. It was ſhagged with wood, and continued va-rying its form, but ſtill preſerving its immen-ſity, through the ſpace of at leaſt two miles. In ſome parts its ſummit beetled frightfully over the river, and gave an involuntary ſhud-der to the paſſenger, as he paſſed under its tre-mendous ſhade.

SECT. XXV.

AS we were leaving Plymouth, the town was greatly agitated with an account received that morning of the battle of Lexington, which happened on the 19th of April. We had been chiefly in company with General Bell of the marines; and as a large detachment from that corps was with the troops in America, the general's houſe was crowded with people inquiring after their relations and friends; while they who looked farther, conceived, that as blood was now drawn, all hope of accommodation was over.

We left Plymouth under the impreſſion of theſe melancholy ideas, till a ſucceſſion of new objects diſlodged them. By the Aſhburton road we took our route to Exeter.

About three miles from Plymouth ſtands Salterham, the ſeat of Mr. Parker. It is Mount Edgcomb in miniature; being ſituated on a

ſmall

fmall peninfula, and furrounded, not indeed by the fea, but by a confiderable creek.

Mr. Parker commands a view of St. Nicholas's ifland, Mount Edgcomb, and the Ram's-head; but though the objects are great, they did not appear to us either picturefque in themfelves, or agreeably combined. The ground, particularly beyond the creek, is ill fhaped.

The foil of Salterham feems as unkindly to vegetation, as Mount Edgcomb is friendly to it; and the creek it ftands on, is entirely forfaken by the tide at ebb, and becomes a mere channel of ooze. Perhaps in our remarks here we were too much under the impreffion of the gloomy ideas we had brought from Plymouth.

From Salterham, we purfued our route to Ivybridge; where, as far as we could judge from the appearance of the river, we fhould have met with fome beautiful fcenery, if we had had time to examine it.

From hence we proceeded to Afhburton, which lies among hills; and Chudleigh, where

are

are ftone-quarries, which at a diftance have the appearance of a grand range of natural rock. Here the bifhops of Exeter formerly refided. The ruins of the epifcopal palace may ftill be traced.

We were but little amufed, however, with any thing we faw in this country. The whole of it from Plymouth is but an uninterefting fcene. Its very appearance on a map, fhews, in fome degree, its unpicturefque form. It is interfected with feveral rivers, which run in vallies between oppofite hills. Thefe hills we were continually afcending or defcending. When we had mounted one hill, we were prefented with the fide of another; fo that all diftance was fhut out, and all variety of country intercepted. A pleafant glade here and there, at the dip of a hill, we fometimes had; but this did not compenfate for that tirefome famenefs of afcent and defcent which runs through the country.

At Chudleigh we left the great Exeter-road, to fee Mamhead, and Powderham-caftle. In our

way

way we mounted a fort of grand natural *ter-race*, about feven miles in length, and three in breadth ; though this indeed is a broader fur-face than we commonly diftinguifh by that ap-pellation. The name of this eminence is Hal-down-hill.

From hence we had a grand, extenfive, and, in many parts, a picturefque diftance ; confift-ing firft of the whole courfe of the Ex, from Exeter to the fea, the city of Exeter, the town of Topfham, Sir Francis Drake's, and Powder-ham-caftle. Beyond thefe objccts, all of which feemed in the diftance to adorn the banks of the river, the eye ranged over immenfe plains and woods, hills and vales. Of thefe the vale of Honiton, and other celebrated vales made a part. But they were mere fpecks, too incon-fiderable for the eye to fix on. Diftance had preffed all the hilly boundaries of thefe vales flat to the furface. At leaft it had fo dimi-nifhed them, that the proudeft appeared only as a ripple on the ocean. The extreme parts of this vaft landfcape were bounded by the long range of Sedbury-hills; which were tinged, when we faw them, with a light ether hue, fcarce one fhade removed from the colour

of

of the fky ; the whole immenfe fcene, therefore, without the leaft interruption from the
hills of the country, faded gradually into air.

A view of this kind gives us a juft idea of
the furface of the globe we inhabit. We talk
of its inequalities in a lofty ftile. Its mountains
afcend the fkies ; its vallies fink down into
depths profound. Whereas, in fact, its inequalities are nothing, when compared with its
magnitude. If a comprehenfive eye, placed at
a diftance from the furface of the earth, were
capable of viewing a whole hemifphere together, all its inequalities, great as we make
them, Mount Caucafus, the Andes, Teneriffe,
and all the loftieft mountains of the globe,
would be compreffed, like the view before us ;
and the whole would appear perfectly fmooth.
To us, a bowling green is a level plain ; but a
minute infect finds it full of inequalities.

In furveying the windings of the Ex, in its
courfe to the fea, we are reminded of a fketch,
by a great mafter, of the courfe of Aufente. It
is flightly touched indeed, but with great fpirit ; and the diftances are particularly well
marked.

marked. We have it at the end of the feventh
Æneid, where the picturefque poet, led by his
fubject to mention fome of the countries of
Italy, gives us this pleafing view :

> —— Queis Jupiter Anxurus arvis
> Præfidet ; et viridi gaudens Feronia luco ;
> Qua Saturæ jacet atra palus; gelidufque per imas
> Quærit iter valles, atque in mare conditur Ufens.

In this landfcape we have firft the fore-ground,
compofed of the Temple of Jupiter Anxur,
proudly feated ; and overlooking the neighbouring country.

> —— Queis Jupiter Anxurus arvis
> Præfidet———

The immediate diftance confifts of the Temple
of Feronia, marked by a grove, which adorns
it, and a lake lying at its foot :

> ——Viridi gaudens Feronia luco ;
> Qua Saturæ jacet atra palus———

The lake to which the poet gives the epithet
atra, had that deep black clear hue, which
Claude and Pouffin well knew produced often
the beft effect. In the fecond diftance all *colour* is gone; and the fading landfcape of courfe
takes its aërial tinge. It is enough now, if a
few principal objects are dimly feen. A winding

ing river is the moſt diſtinguiſhable. It is diſ-
covered only by its meanders along the plain ;

> ——Geliduſque per imas
> Quærit iter valles——

It has not its courſe ſhaped out between high
banks, but *ſeeks out* its paſſage, here and there,
as the ſmall depreſſions of a flat country allow.
Beyond all appears the ſea ; but the diſtance
here is ſo remote, that it is not marked with
any degree of ſtrength : no epithet is applied :
you can ſcarce diſtinguiſh it from the ſky.
Criticiſms of this kind may ſeem refinement ;
but there is little doubt, I think, but the poet,
in compoſing theſe lines, had ſome real landſcape ſtrongly formed in his imagination.
Chance could not have marked all theſe diſtances ſo very exactly.

Having deſcended Haldown-hill, we ſaw
Mamhead, the ſeat of Lord Liſburne, and
Powderham-caſtle ; though we had no time to
examine either.

The former from a woody hill, which ſeems
to be adorned with much beautiful ſcenery,
commands a noble view over the mouth of the
Ex. The latter ſtands on a knoll, overlooking
a flat

a flat park, bounded by the fame river; but with a lefs amufing view of it. The Ex in both thefe views is a grand tide channel; and in the former efpecially is very beautiful. But we faw nothing in the diftance either from Mamhead, or Powderham-caftle, which Haldown-hill had not already fhewn us, though not in all refpects perhaps to fo much advantage.

S E C T. XXVI.

THE city of Exeter, which we foon reached, is by far the moft confiderable town in the weft of England. It is feated rather eminently on the eaftern fide of the Ex. From this river it derives its name; which is a corruption of Ex-cefter, or the caftle on the Ex; a name which gives it a title to Roman origin. The anti-quarian, however, is not obliged merely to ety-mology for his proof of its antiquity. He points out veftiges of Roman mafonry in the fouth gate; he finds variety of coins; and he meafures the length and breadth of the walls, which form a parallelogram by Roman feet.

Exeter is faid to be very regularly built, having two large airy ftreets, running through the length and breadth of it, and uniting in the centre. It appeared to us, however, very in-cumbered. We were directed from the bridge to the great church through clofe and difagree-able alleys. The beft part of the town we did not fee; as our time allowed us to examine only the moft remarkable buildings.

2   On

On the north side, the higheſt ground is occupied by the ruins of Rugement-caſtle, formerly the reſidence of Saxon kings. From the terrace of this caſtle, and from the walls of the town, we had the ſame extenſive view over the country, which we had before from Haldown-hill: but as we now ſaw them from a different ſtation, and from a lower point, they were leſs grand, but more picturesque. Hills which were there compreſſed to the ſurface, began here to ariſe, and take their form in the landſcape; breaking the continued lines of diſtance, and creating new lights, and new ſhades with their varied elevations. Towards the mouth of the river, we were told, a light miſt often prevails, when the reſt of the landſcape towards the weſt is perfectly clear. We did not ſee any appearance of this kind; but I ſhould ſuppoſe it might frequently produce a good effect, not only from the beauty of the miſt itſelf, but from its clearing away *, and leaving ſome objects diſtinctly ſeen, and others but obſcurely traced.

The good Biſhop Rundle, who was educated in this town, ſpeaks with picturesque warmth

---

* See page 162.

of

of the views from its public walks, and the great beauty of the landfcape around it. The climate he affirms to be fo fine, that in no part of England trees fhoot with more luxuriance, or fruits ripen to a richer flavour. The fig and the grape, he fays, fcarce defire better fkies *.

Few places in England are more renowned in the annals of war, than Exeter. It was three times befieged by the Danes, once by William the Conqueror, again by King Stephen, a fixth time in the rebellion of Perkin Warbec in the time of Henry VII. again in a rebellion which broke out in the reign of Edward VI. and two or three times more in the civil wars of Charles I. On many of thefe occafions it was regularly garrifoned; and the citizens had nothing to do with its defence. But when it refted on *them*, they generally behaved with remarkable fpirit. Many inftances of their gallantry are preferved in hiftory. Henry VII. was fo much pleafed with their behaviour, in his time, that he paid them a vifit on purpofe to thank them; and when he left the town, he took his fword from his fide, and prefenting it

* See Letters of the late T. Rundle, LL.D.

to

to the Mayor, defired it might always be carried before him; which it has been ever fince.

The hiftory of the great church at Exeter
is remarkable. It was four hundred years in
building, under the direction of feveral bifhops;
each adding fomething to complete the defign;
one of them even lengthened the nave of the
church by two additional arches. Yet notwithftanding this lapfe of time, in which the
fafhion of architecture underwent fo much
change; and notwithftanding the different architects employed, whofe genius and tafte muft
have been very different, it is fingular, that
each fucceeding bifhop hath fo attentively purfued the plan of his predeceffor, that the whole
together ftrikes the eye as a uniform building.
On examining the parts nicely, we may here
and there diftinguifh the oppofition of Saxon
and Gothic; but, in general, they accord very
happily. The weft front is uncommonly rich,
and adorned with figures. The nave of the
church is fitted up for divine fervice; which
may be ufeful, but injures the effect.

The curious fhould not forget, before he
leave the church, to fee the chalice and fap-
phire ring, which were dug out of a bifhop's
grave, when a new pavement was laid about
twenty

twenty years ago. To what bishop the ring belonged is only guessed; but it might be tolerably ascertained by a knowledge of the progress of art which some antiquarians possess. Such a knowledge gives the form and workmanship of these curious remains of antiquity to their proper period. If the traveller have a mind also to please his conductor, who leads him through the aisles of the church, he may tell him, he has heard that the great bell, called Peter, weighs above a thousand pounds more than Great Tom at Lincoln; and that the pipes of the organ are wider than those of any organ in Europe. Both these accounts he will probably hear confirmed with great solemnity, though the latter of them is a mistake; and as to the former, both it and its rival at Lincoln are mere hand-bells compared with the great bell at Moscow, which weighs 432,000 pounds, and measures at its mouth above twenty-one yards.

SECT. XXVII.

FROM Exeter to Honiton we paffed through a rich country, yet fomewhat flatter than we had met with on the weftern fide of Exeter. We found, however, here and there, an eminence, which gave us a view of the diftances around. At Fair-mile-hill, particularly, a very *extenfive* view opened before us ; but nothing can make it pleafing, as it is *bounded by a hard edge*. A diftance fhould either melt into the fky, or terminate in a foft and varied mountain line *.

This high ground, which appeared at a *diftance* as a *hard edge*, is on the fpot a grand terrace, running eight or nine miles from Honiton to Sidmouth, prefenting fometimes the fea, and fometimes a variety of hills, vales, and diftances, with which the country abounds. We had not time, however, to explore the feveral beauties of the landfcape it overlooks. Night came on before we reached Honiton, and drew a veil over all the objects of the horizon.

* See page 29.

At

At Honiton we intended to sleep; but it was ordered otherwise. This town having been twice burnt down within these last thirty years, the inhabitants take a very effectual method to prevent the catastrophe a third time, by appointing all travellers to the office of watchmen. About twelve o'clock a fellow begins his operations with a monstrous hand-bell, and a hoarse voice, informing us, that all is safe. This serenade is repeated every quarter of an hour, with great propriety; for in that portion of time, it may reasonably be supposed the traveller, who is ignorant of the institution, and not accustomed to such nocturnal-din in a country-town, cannot well get his senses composed, especially as his ear will naturally lie in expectation of each periodical peal. In the mean time, the sly inhabitant, who is used to these noises of the night, enjoys a quiet repose. The institution may be good: we only wished it had been intimated to us before, that we might have had an option in the case.

We had now travelled between seventy and eighty miles from Plymouth, and found the whole of the country, (except the little devi-ation

ation we made from Chudleigh, to examine the scenery about the Ex,) unvaried and uninteresting. Like an immense piece of high furrowed land, at least as far as Exeter, it is continually rising and falling; and though it has its beauties, yet they are chiefly seen near the coast, where its vallies break down, and open to the sea; and where its estuaries often form very pleasing scenes.

The road from Plymouth to Honiton, by the *sea-coast*, was the road we ought to have taken ; but as it had not been pointed out to us as particularly picturesque, we took the upper road merely for want of better information. I shall, however, give the reader a sketch of the *coast*, from some hints which I have had on good picturesque authority. I have also myself seen a great variety of accurate drawings of this coast, which have given me a strong idea of its character.

S E C T. XXVIII.

FROM Plymouth, according to this route, you make the firſt ſtage to Totneſs; and ſo far the country wears nearly the ſame face which it did between Plymouth and Aſh-burton. You croſs the ſame rivers, aſcend the ſame hills, and fall into the ſame vallies.

This is a country, however, in which the farmer glories; though the painter treats it with neglect. Here the acre fills the buſhel with abundant increaſe; and here the ox does credit to his paſture. But though the country abounds in corn and paſturage, cyder is its ſtaple. The cyder of the South Hams, which is the name of a great part of this country, is every where famous.

At Totneſs you meet the Dart; down which river you may ſail, about ſix or ſeven miles, to Dartmouth. This little navigation I have heard much extolled as a peculiar ſcene of beauty; but I have heard others on whoſe judgment I can more rely, ſpeak of it with leſs emotion. And yet I can eaſily imagine,

3   that

that two people of equally picturesque taste, may conceive differently of the same scene. They may have different conceptions of beauty, though the conceptions of each may be very just; or they may examine the same scene under different circumstances. A favourable, or an unfavourable light makes a greater alteration in any scene, than a person unaccustomed to examine nature would easily imagine.

At Dartmouth you have a great variety of interesting views. The bay, which the river forms at its mouth, is one of the most beautiful scenes on the coast. Both the entrance of the Dart into it, and its exit to the sea, appear from many stations closed up by the folding of the banks; so that the bay has frequently the form of a lake, only furnished with shipping instead of boats. Its banks are its great beauty; which consist of lofty wooded hills, shelving down in all directions. You would not expect such scenery on a sea-coast: but the woods by being well sheltered grow luxuriantly.

And yet an eye versed in the various scenes of nature, would easily distinguish these bays from the pastoral simplicity of an inland-lake. The sea always impresses a peculiar character on its bays. The water has a different aspect;

its

its tints are more varied, and its furface differently difturbed. Its banks too have a more
weather-beaten and ragged appearance, lofing
generally their verdure within the air of the
fea. The fea-rock alfo wants that rich incruf-
tation of moffes and lychens, which adorns the
rock of the lake; and the wood, though it
grow luxuriantly, as it does here, fhews plainly
by its mode of growth, that it is the inhabitant
of a fea-girt clime. To this may be added,
that the appendages of the bay and lake are different. A quay perhaps for landing goods,
an anchor, a floating buoy, or a group of
figures in feamen's jackets, are the ornaments
of one fcene, but unknown to the other.

The bay, in the mean time, may be as picturefque as the lake. All I mean to point out
is, that the *character* of each is different; and
therefore in painting they fhould not be confounded. Its *particular value* each receives
from the fancy of the fpectator. As was juft
obferved, people may have different conceptions of beauty, and yet the conceptions of both
may be equally juft. The paftoral fimplicity
of the lake may pleafe one perfon, and the
buftle of the bay another. I fhall only add,
that reprefentations of the two fcenes are exceedingly

ceedingly well fuited as companions to each other.

At the opening of Dartmouth-bay to the fea, appears the town of Dartmouth, afcending a hill. Its caftle, at the diftance of a mile, ftands clofe to the water's edge. On the other fide, acrofs the bay, rifes Kingfwere, a fort of fuburb, belonging to the town. The winding of the bay, and the varied beauty of its banks are feen to great advantage in a walk which carries you from the town of Dartmouth to the caftle.

All this coaft affords excellent fifh. The fole breeds here in great abundance, and the john dory delights in it, as its moft favourite haunt. The Torbay-boat often brings this delicious fifh to the tables of the luxurious: but the epicure, who wifhes to eat it in per-fection, does not think a journey to thefe coafts too much. At Totnefs great quantities of falmon-peal are taken in an uncommon mode of fifhing. The fifh are intercepted, as the water ebbs, by dogs, which fwim-ming after the fhoal, are taught to drive them up the river into clofe nets provided to receive them.

Dart-

Dartmouth harbour is a very bufy fcene when a fhoal of pilchards enters it, as they often do at particular feafons, driven in by porpoifes, which lie off at fea in expectation of them. The fhoal difcovers itfelf by the tremulous motion of the water, and the leaping of the fifh here and there on the furface. On this appearance every boat that can fwim, puts off from the fhore with nets. The whole would make a bufy and entertaining water fcene, if it were well painted.

From Dartmouth you return with the tide tide to Totnefs. From thence, in the way to Brixham, you may vifit the grand ruins of Berry-Pomeroy-caftle. This fortrefs belonged formerly to a family of the name of Pomeroy ; which being feated there by the Conqueror, kept poffeffion of it, during all the various revolutions of England, till the reign of Edward VI. It was once a formidable place; and its ruins are ftill magnificent. The grand gate-way remains entire, together with a round tower. A great part of the wall is ftanding, and many of the chambers may be traced.

From hence you proceed to Brixham, where the naturalift finds himfelf puzzled with a well, which

which ebbs and flows, though the waters are not in the leaft brackifh, but pure and limpid, which feems to indicate they have no communication with tides.

Near Brixham you begin to fkirt that celebrated inlet of the fea, called Torbay. It is a grand fcene, and affords many magnificent views, if you have leifure to circle the bay in queft of them.

Its general form is femilunar, inclofing a circumference of about twelve miles. Its winding fhores on both fides are fkreened with grand ramparts of rock; between which, in the central part, the ground from the country, forming a gentle vale, falls eafily to the water's edge. Wood grows all round the bay, even on its *rocky fides*, where it can get footing, and fhelter; but in the *central part* with great luxuriance.

In this delicious fpot ftood formerly Torabbey, the ruins of which ftill remain. Its fituation was grand and beautiful. Wooded hills, defcending on every fide, fkreened and adorned it both behind and on its flanks. In front the bay opening before it, fpread its circling rocky cheeks, like a vaft colonade, leffening in all the pleafing forms of perfpective; and receiving

all

all the variety of light and fhade, which the fun veering round from morning till evening, throws upon them. Here a fociety of monks dwelt in peaceful fecurity. The enemy's fleet more than once, in former times, ravaged the coaft, and burnt Dartmouth and other towns. The abbey feared no mifchief. All it had to do, was to open its hofpitable gates, and give an afylum to the terrified fugitives of the country.

This noble bay has afforded its protection many a time to the fleets of England, which in their full array ride fafely within its ample bafon. But it appeared in its greateft glory on the fifth of November 1688, when King William entered it with fifty fail of the line, and four hundred tranfports. The fhips indeed were Dutch; but a Britifh admiral led the van, and a Britifh flag flew at the maft-head.

From Torbay your next ftage is Newton-Bufhel, where, croffing the Teign, you ride along the banks of that river to Teign-mouth. In your way you are entertained with a variety of river views. But Nature, laying afide here in a great degree her rocks and bold fhores, works with fofter materials. The banks of the
Teign,

Teign, I underſtand, are rather cultivated than wild ; though at its mouth it receives the ſea with rocks, which are both magnificent and beautiful. They are covered, like the generality of the rocks on this coaſt, with a profuſion of wood.

From Teign-mouth you ſkirt the ſhore to the mouth of the Ex, over which you ferry at the bar. Here the country grows ſomewhat bolder, but rather in the form of ſwelling hills. Theſe hills likewiſe are profuſely covered with wood, which ſweeps almoſt down to the water's edge. But as you take a view of them with your back to the ſea, they appear in ſtill greater magnificence, uniting with the woods of the country. Thoſe of Powderham-caſtle receive them firſt ; and beyond theſe you ſee riſing and ſtretching into diſtance the woods of Mam-head, in rich, though indiſtinct, luxuriance.

The Ex is by far the nobleſt river in this part of the coaſt. It empties a profuſe channel into the ſea, and forms a baſon at its mouth, which would be an excellent harbour for a royal navy, if it were not obſtructed by a bar. When the tide flows, however, ſhips of conſiderable burthen advance as far as Topſham, and could formerly have proceeded with equal

eaſe

eafe to the walls of Exeter; but a little above Topfham the channel of the river is again obftructed.

The tradition of the country afcribes this obftruction to a quarrel between the Mayor of Exeter, and an Earl of Devonfhire. The earl claimed the firft falmon that was taken in the feafon, as an acknowledgment of his jurifdiction over the river. The mayor claimed it as a perquifite of his office. The earl's claim appears to have been worfe founded; becaufe, inftead of appealing to the laws for redrefs, he had recourfe to private revenge. Both fides of the river were his property; and both fides clofely wooded with ancient oak. Thefe trees he cut down in abundance, and threw them into the channel of the river. The tide afterwards carrying up with it great quantities of fand and gravel, formed this obftruction by degrees into fuch a barrier, as could never afterwards be removed. If this tradition be well grounded, we have feldom an inftance of revenge in fo grand a ftyle. Moft people, who feek gratifications of this kind, are fatisfied with revenging themfelves on the perfon who had offended them. But the Earl of Devonfhire not only revenged himfelf on the Mayor

of

of Exeter ; but on the whole city, and for all future times.

About feventy years ago the inhabitants of Exeter cut a new channel for the river, and built very expenfive locks upon it; by means of which they can now bring veffels of fome burthen to the town.

From the mouth of the Ex the coaft affords nothing very interefting, till you come to the mouth of the Sid. This river opens into the fea between high promontories ; that on the weft is particularly lofty, and much broken, though not rocky, and is reprefented as affording many picturefque views. But here is no bafon opening into the land, as in the other rivers of this coaft. The Sid is a mere rural ftream, and preferves its character pure to the very fhores of the ocean.

The valley through which it takes its courfe, is a fcene of peculiar conftruction. It forms a gentle defcent towards the fea between two fteep hills which leave little more room at the bottom, than what the road and the river occupy. So that, in fact, it has hardly the dimenfions of a valley, but might rather be called a cleft in the higher grounds, running down to the fea. The hills, however, which

compofe

compofe its fides, are not (like the narrow
vallies of a mountainous and rocky country) abrupt and broken; but confift chiefly of rich
pafturage, and are covered with flocks and
herds. They are adorned too with wood; and
though in their courfe they now and then wind
a little, they generally lead the valley in a
ftraight line from north to fouth.

Through this narrow valley you rife flowly
near the fpace of nine miles. So long an afcent, though in all parts gradual, raifes you at
length to a great height. At the conclufion of
the valley, you find yourfelf on a lofty down;
from whence you have fome of the grandeft
views which this country, rich in diftances,
affords. You look chiefly towards the weft,
and take in an amazing compafs; indeed all
the diftrict on both fides of the Ex, as far as
the fea. Thefe high grounds formed that *hard
edge*, and made that peculiar appearance, which
we obferved in the road between Exeter and
Honiton*. From thefe lofty downs you defcend gently into Honiton, where thefe two
different routes from Plymouth unite.

* See page 225.

SECT. XXIX.

AS we left Honiton, the obſcurity of a hazy morning overſpread its vale; the pictu-reſque beauty of which we had heard much commended. If, therefore, it poſſeſſes any, (which from the analogy of the country may be queſtioned,) we are not qualified to give any account of it. A miſty morning, in gene-ral, gives new beauty to a country; but we muſt catch its beautiful appearance, as we do all the other *accidental* appearances of Nature, at a proper criſis. We left Honiton at too early an hour in the morning to ſee the full effect of the miſt. It rather blotted out, than adorned, the face of the country. The moſt picturesque moment of a miſty morning is juſt as the ſun riſes, and begins its contention with the vapours which obſtruct its rays. That ap-pearance we had ſoon after, and in ſuch profu-ſion, that it gave a beautiful effect to a land-ſcape, which ſeemed not calculated to produce much effect without it.

We

We have a ftriking picture of a morning-fun, though unaccompanied by mift, in the fhort account given us of Lot's efcape from Sodom. We are told, *The fun was rifen upon the earth, when Lot entered into Zoar.* Defcriptive poetry and painting muft both have *objects of fenfe* before them. Neither of them deals in *abftracted ideas.* But the fame objects will not always fuit both. Images, which may fhine under the poet's defcription, are not perhaps at the fame time picturefque; though I believe every picturefque object is capable of fhining as a poetical one. The paffage before us is both poetical and picturefque. A relation of the plain fact would have been neither. If the paffage had been coldly tranflated, *Lot arrived at Zoar about fun-rife;* the fenfe had been preferved, but the picture would have been loft. As it is tranflated, the whole is imagery. The firft part of the expreffion, *the fun was rifen upon the earth,* brings immediately before the eye, (through the *connection* of the fun and the earth,) the rays of a morning fun ftriking the tops of the hills and promontories; while the other part of the expreffion, *Lot entered into Zoar,* brings before us (through the fame

happy

happy mode of raising and connecting images)
a road, the gates of the town, and the patriarch
approaching it. Not, by the way, that we should
wish to introduce the *story* of Lot's retreat,
with any *diftinction* into the picture. The principal part would be the *landscape*; and Lot
could only be a diftant figure to adorn it, and
in that light unneceffary. *Hiftory* introduced
as the *ornament of landscape* appears abfurd.
In Baffon, and fome other mafters, fuch intro-
ductions are frequent. We confider, therefore, the paffage before us merely as *landscape*,
and lay little ftrefs on the *figures*. Reubens
has thrown a fine glow of colouring into a
picture on this fubject, in the poffeffion of the
Duke of Marlbrough. But Reubens has introduced, as he ought, the figures on the *foreground*, making the landscape entirely an *un-
der-part*. I forget whether he has given his
picture the full effect it might receive by
throwing the back fcenery into that grand
fhade, fuggefted by the words of fcripture, the
*fmoke of the country went up as the fmoke of a
furnace*. The atmofphere alfo might have a
good effect, tinged with the ruddy glare of fire
blended with the fmoke.

As

As the mift cleared away, and we faw more of the country around, its picturefque charms did not increafe upon us. If the hills and dales, however, of which the whole country is compofed, poffefs little of this kind of beauty, they poffefs what is better, the riches of foil, and cultivation in a high degree. If any vallies can be faid to *laugh and fing*, thefe certainly may. Nothing can exceed either their tillage or their pafturage.

Among the beautiful objects we occafionally met with in this country, the cattle, which every where grazed its rich paftures, were worthy of remark. Moft of thofe we faw feemed to be of a peculiar breed, elegantly and neatly formed, rather fmall, generally red, growing gradually darker towards the head and fhoulders. Their horns, which are fhort, are tipped with black; their coats are fine, and their heads fmall.

At Axminfter the carpet-works are worth vifiting. Some of them difplay a very rich combination of colours; but in general, they are fo gay, that furniture muft be glaring to be

in

in harmony with them. Of courfe they are too gay to be beautiful.

No carpeting, perhaps, equals the Perfian in beauty. The Turkey carpet is modeft enough in its colouring; but its texture is coarfe, and its pattern confifts commonly of fuch a jumble of incoherent parts, that the eye feldom traces any meaning in its plan. The Britifh carpet again has *too much meaning.* It often repre-fents fruits, and flowers, and bafkets, and other things, which are generally ill reprefented, or awkwardly larger than the life, or at leaft im-properly placed under our feet. The Perfian carpet avoids thefe two extremes. It feldom exhibits any *real forms*, and yet, inftead of the diforderly pattern that deforms the Turkey carpet, it ufually prefents fome neat and ele-gant plan, within the compartments of which its colours, though rich, are modeft. The tex-ture alfo of the carpet is as neat and elegant as the ornamental fcrawl which adorns it.

T

SECT. XXX.

FROM Axminſter we left the great road to
viſit Ford-abbey.

In a ſequeſtered part of the country, where
Devonſhire and Dorſetſhire unite, lies a circular valley, about a mile and half in diameter.

Its ſides ſlope gently into its area in various
directions; but are no where ſteep. Woody
ſkreens, circling its precincts, conceal its bounds;
and in many parts connecting with the trees,
which deſcend into the boſom of the valley,
form themſelves into various tufted groves.
Through the middle of this ſweet retreat winds
a ſtream, not foaming among broken rocks, nor
ſounding down cataracts; but mild like the
ſcene it accompanies, and in cadence not ex-
ceeding a gentle murmur. From this retreat
all foreign ſcenery is excluded. It wants no
adventitious ornaments; ſufficiently bleſſed
with its own ſweet groves and ſolitude.

——Such *landſcape*
Needs not the foreign aid of ornament;
But is, when unadorned, adorned the moſt.

This

This happy retirement was once sacred to religion. Verging towards one side of the valley stand the ruins of Ford-abbey. It has never been of large dimensions, but was a model of the most perfect Gothic, if we may credit its remains, particularly those of a cloister, which are equal to any thing we have in that style of architecture. This beautiful fragment consists of eight windows, with light buttresses between them, and joins a ruined chapel on one side, and on the other a hall or refectory, which still preserves its form sufficiently to give an idea of its just proportions. To this is connected by ruined walls a massy tower. What the ancient use of this fabric was, whether it belonged to the ecclesiastical or civil part of the monastery, is not now apparent; but at present it gives a picturesque form to the ruin, which appears to more advantage by the pre-eminence of some superior part*.

At right angles with the chapel runs another cloister, a longer building, but of coarser workmanship, and almost covered with ivy. The river, which enters the valley at the distance of about half a mile from the ruin, takes

* See page 135.

T 2

a sweep

a fweep towards it, and paffing under this cloifter, opens into what was once the great court,
and makes its exit through an arch in the
wall on the oppofite fide.

This venerable pile,
——clad in the moffy veft of fleeting time,

and decorated all over with variety of lychens,
ftreaming weather-ftains, and twifting fhrubs,
is fhaded by ancient oaks, which, hanging over
it, adorn its broken walls without encumbering
them. In fhort, the valley, the river, the path,
and the ruins are all highly pleafing; the *parts*
are beautiful, and the *whole* is harmonious.

They who have lately feen Ford-abbey will
ftare at this defcription of it. And well may
they ftare; for this defcription antedates its
prefent ftate by at leaft a century. If they had
feen it in the year 1675, they might probably
have feen it as it is here defcribed. Now, alas!
it wears another face. It has been in the hands
of *improvement*. Its fimplicity is gone; and
miferable ravage has been made through every
part. The ruin is patched up into an awkward
dwelling; old parts and new are blended together, to the mutual difgrace of both. The elegant cloifter is ftill left; but it is completely
repaired,

repaired, white-wafhed, and converted into a green-houfe. The hall too is modernized, and every other part. Safh-windows glare over pointed arches, and Gothic walls are adorned with Indian paper.

The grounds have undergone the fame reformation. The natural groves and lawns are deftroyed; viftas and regular flopes fupply their room. The winding path, which contemplation naturally marked out, is gone; fucceeded by ftraight walks, and terraces adorned with urns and ftatues; while the river and its fringed banks have given way to canals and ftew-ponds. In a word, a fcene abounding with fo many natural beauties was never perhaps more wretchedly deformed.

When a man exercifes his crude ideas on a few vulgar acres, it is of little confequence. The injury is eafily repaired; and if not, the lofs is trifling. But when he lets loofe his depraved tafte, his abfurd invention, and his gracelefs hands on fuch a fubject as this, where art and nature united cannot reftore the havoc he makes, we confider fuch a deed under the fame black character in matters of picturefque beauty, as we do facrilege and blafphemy in matters of religion. The effects of fuperftition

we

we abhor. Some little atonement, however,
this implacable power might have made in
taſte, for its miſchiefs in religion, if it had de-
terred our anceſtors from connecting their
manſions with ruins once dedicated to ſacred
uſes. We might then have enjoyed in perfection many noble ſcenes, which are now
either entirely effaced or miſerably mangled.

Before we leave theſe ſcenes, I muſt relate a
ſtory of the monks of Ford, which does great
credit to their piety. It happened (in what
century tradition ſays not) that a gentleman of
the name of Courtney, a benefactor to the
abbey, was overtaken at ſea by a violent ſtorm;
and the ſeamen having toiled many hours in
vain, and being entirely ſpent, abandoned
themſelves to deſpair. " My good lads," (ſaid
Courtney, calling them together, and pulling
out his watch, if watches were then in uſe,)
" My good lads, you ſee it is now four o'clock.
" At five we ſhall certainly be relieved. At
" that hour the monks of Ford riſe to their de-
" votions, and in their prayers to St. Francis,
" will be ſure to remember me among their
" benefactors; and you will have the benefit
" of being ſaved in my company. Perſevere
" only one hour, and you may depend on
" what

" what I fay." This fpeech reanimated the whole crew. Some flew to the pump, others to the leak; all was life and fpirit. By this vigorous effort, at five o'clock the fhip was fo near the fhore, that fhe eafily reached it ; and St. Francis got all the credit of the efcape.

S E C T. XXXI.

FROM Ford-abbey we were obliged to return to Axminfter, and from thence we fet
out for Bridport, traverfing vaft cultivated hills,
from which, on the left, we had views into the
country, and on the right, over the fea. The
ifle of Portland ranged in the diftance, many
leagues along the fhore, forming a long white
beach; which made an uncommon appearance.

From Bridport to Dorchefter we paffed
through a more inland country, though in
other refpects fimilar to the country we had
juft left. The features of it are broad and
determined. Sweeping hills with harfh edges
interfect each other. Here and there a bottom is cultivated, inclofed, and adorned with a
farm-houfe and a few trees; but, in general,
the whole country is an extended down. It
is every where fed with little rough fheep;
which have formed it, with conftant grazing,
into the fineft pafturage. Indeed a chalky foil
itfelf, which is the fubftratum of thefe downs,

is

is naturally inclined to produce a neat fmooth
furface. The feveral flocks which pafture thefe
wide domains, have their refpective walks;
and are generally found within the diftance of
a mile from each other. We faw them once
or twice iffuing from their pens, to take their
morning's repaft after a hungry night. It
was a pleafing fight to fee fuch numbers of in-
nocent animals made happy, and in the following lines it is beautifully defcribed:

————The fold
Poured out its fleecy tenants o'er the glebe.
At firft, progreffive as a ftream, they fought
The middle field; but fcattered by degrees
In various groups, they whitened all the land.

But the progreffive motion here defcribed,
is one of thofe incidents, which is a better fubject for poetry than painting. For, in the firft
place, a *feeding flock* is feldom well *grouped*;
they commonly *feparate*; or, as the poet well
expreffes it, *they are fcattered by degrees, and
whiten all the land.* Nor are their attitudes
varied, as they all ufually move the fame way,
progreffive like a ftream. Indeed the fhape of
a *feeding fheep* is not the moft pleafing, as its
back and neck make a round heavy line, which
in contraft only has its effect. To fee a flock
of

of fheep in their moft picturefque form, we fhould fee them repofing after their meal is over; and if they are in funfhine, they are ftill the more beautiful. In *repofing* they are generally better grouped, and their forms are more varied. Some are commonly ftanding, and others lying on the ground, with their little ruminating heads in various forms. And if the light be ftrong, it fpreads over the whole one general mafs; and is contrafted, at the fame time, by a fhadow equally ftrong, which the flock throws upon the ground. It may be obferved alfo, that the fleece itfelf is well difpofed to receive a beautiful effect of light. It does not indeed, like the fmooth covering of hair, allow the eye to trace the mufcular form of the animal. But it has a beauty of a different kind: the flakinefs of the wool catches the light, and breaking it into many parts, yet without deftroying the mafs, gives it a peculiar richnefs.

We faw another circumftance alfo, in which fheep appear to advantage. The weather was fultry, the day calm, and the roads dufty. Along thefe roads we faw, once or twice, a flock of fheep driven, which raifed a confiderable cloud. As we were a little higher on the downs,

downs, and not annoyed by the duſt, the circumſtance was amuſing. The beauty of the
incident lay in the contraſt between ſuch ſheep
as were *ſeen perfectly*, and ſuch as were *involved in obſcurity*. At the ſame time the duſt
became a kind of harmonizing medium, which
united the flock into one whole. It had the
ſame effect on a group of animals, which a
heavy miſt, when partial, has on landſcape.
But though circumſtances of this kind are
pleaſing in nature, we do not wiſh to ſee them
imitated on canvas. They have been tried by
Loutherberg, who with a laudable endeavour
hath attempted many different *effects*; but I
think in this he has failed. He has repreſented the duſty atmoſphere of rapid wheels.
But it is an incident that cannot be imitated:
for, as motion enters neceſſarily into the idea,
and as you cannot deſcribe motion, it is impoſ-
ſible to give more than half the idea. It is
otherwiſe with vapour, which, from the *light
miſt* to the *ſleeping fog*, is of a more perma-
nent nature, and therefore more adapted to the
pencil.

The only circumſtance which can make a
cloud of duſt an object of imitation, is *diſtance*;
as this gives it ſomewhat of a ſtationary appearance.

pearance. One of the grandeſt ideas of this
kind, which I remember to have met with, may
be found in Zenophon's Anabaſis.

As Cyrus was approaching Artaxerxes over
one of thoſe vaſt plains which are often found
in the eaſt, a horſeman, who had been making
obſervations, returned at full ſpeed, crying out
to the troops, as he rode through them, that
the enemy was at hand. Cyrus, not ſuſpecting
the king to be ſo near, was riding careleſsly in
his chariot; and the troops unarmed, were
marching negligently over the plain. The
prince, leaping from his chariot, preſently
armed himſelf, mounted his horſe, called his
generals around him, and drew up his troops.
This was ſcarce done, when the hiſtorian tells
us, " a white cloud was ſeen in the diſtant ho-
" rizon ſpreading far and wide, from the duſt
" raiſed by ſo vaſt a hoſt. As the cloud ap-
" proached, the bottom of it appeared dark and
" ſolid. As it ſtill advanced, it was obſerved,
" from various parts, to gleam and glitter in
" the ſun; and ſoon after, the ranks of horſe
" and foot, and armed chariots, were diſtinctly
" ſeen *."

* As the tranſlation is not *exactly* faithful, the critical reader
may be better pleaſed perhaps with the greater ſimplicity of the
original. Εφανη Κονιορτῷ, &c. p. 109, vol. i. Edit. Glaſg.

The

The extended plains of Dorfetfhire, however defolate they now appear, have once been bufy fcenes. The antiquarian finds rich employment among them for his curiofity. To follow him in queft of every heaving hilloc, and to hear a difcuffion of conjectures about the traces of a Danifh or a Roman mattoc, where the eye of common obfervation perceives no traces at all, might be tedious; but he fhews us feveral fragments of antiquity on thefe plains, which are truly curious; and convinces us, that few places in England have been more confiderable in Roman times than Dorchefter. Poundbury and Maiden-caftle, as they are called, are both extraordinary remains of Roman ftations; the latter efpecially, which encompaffes a large fpace of ground. Numberlefs tumuli alfo are thrown up all over the downs. Thefe were antiquities in the times even of the Romans themfelves.

But the moft valuable fragment on thefe plains, is a Roman amphitheatre, about half a mile from Dorchefter. It is conftructed only of earth; but it is of fo firm a texture, that it retains its complete form to this day. Its mounds are of immenfe thicknefs, and feem to be at leaft twenty feet high. The area contains
tains

tains about an acre of land, and is now a corn field. There are two openings in the mound oppofed to each other, which have formerly been gates. The circumference without, appears circular to the eye, though, in fact, I believe it is rather oval; the infide is *apparently* fo. The difference of the figure feems to have been occafioned by the fwelling of the mound within, where the feats have been difpofed. This piece of antiquity is known by the name of *Maumbery*. How much it refembles in form and fize the old amphitheatres now fubfifting in Italy, may be feen from the following defcription of one near Nice. " I made a fe-" cond excurfion to thefe ancient ruins, and " meafured the area of the amphitheatre with " thread. It is an oval figure, the longeft dia-" meter extending about a hundred and thir-" teen yards, and the fhorteft about eighty. " In the centre of it was a fquare ftone, with " an iron ring, to which I fuppofe the wild " beafts were tied, to prevent their fpringing " upon the fpectators. Some of the feats re-" main, with two oppofite entrances, confifting " each of one large gate, and two fmaller late-" ral doors, arched: there is alfo a confider-" able portion of the external wall; but no " columns

" columns or other ornaments of architec-
" ture *."

On comparing the amphitheatre of Dorchefter with this at Nice, we find the form of both
exactly fimilar; and no great difference in the
fize. The area of Maumbery is two hundred
and eighteen feet, by a hundred and fixty-
three. Dr. Stukely calculates, that it might
have contained about thirteen thoufand people.
At Mrs. Canning's execution, who was burnt
in the middle of this amphitheatre for the
murder of her hufband, it is fuppofed to have
contained in the area, and on the mounds, at
leaft ten thoufand fpectators. It is furprifing
that Camden takes not the leaft notice of this
fingular piece of antiquity.

Dorchefter, as we may judge from thefe noble remains, was a place of great confideration
in Roman times. The works of Maiden-caftle,
fuppofed to be capable of receiving fifteen
thoufand men, fhew plainly the confequence
of this ftation in a military light; and I know
not, that the erection of an amphitheatre was
thought neceffary in any other part of Britain;
at leaft we have not, that I recollect, the re-

* See Smollett's Letters.

mains

mains of any other that is well afcertained, except that at Sylchefter.

The fituation of Dorchefter is pleafant. It ftands on a high bank of the Frome, and is furrounded with dry fheep-downs, on which, however, the plough has lately made large encroachments. The town is clean, and well built; and round it is a variety of pleafant walks, which, to a certain degree, I think, fhould always engage the attention of the magiftrate.

In the neighbourhood of Dorchefter are many gentlemen's feats, well worth vifiting. The woody dips among thefe downy hills afford naturally very fine fituations. The only one, however, which we regretted our not being able to fee, was Milton-abbey, the feat of Lord Milton, which lies about three miles from Dorchefter. The day which we had laid out for feeing it was rainy, and we had not time to wait for a better. The capital feature of the landfcape, we were told, is a valley winding among hills of various forms, and covered with woods, which fometimes advance boldly on projecting knolls; and fome-

2   times

times retire in bays and receffes. We heard alfo the ruins of the abbey-church commended, as remains of the pureft Gothic. All thefe materials are in a high degree picturefque; and if they are happily united, Milton-abbey muft be a very interefting fcene. To make a good picture, compofition, however, is as neceffary as pleafing objects.

S E C T. XXXII.

BLANDFORD, our next ſtage, lies about ſixteen miles from Dorcheſter; and, though not a place of ſuch renowned antiquity, is perhaps a ſtill more agreeable town. It lies within a curve of the river Stour, and is pleaſantly ſeated among meadows and woods. If a perſon wiſhed to retire from buſineſs, where he might have the conveniences and pleaſures of the town and country united, his choice might waver between Barnſtaple, Dorcheſter, and Blandford. If he wiſhed to be near the ſea, he will find a pleaſant ſea-coaſt at Barnſtaple. If airy downs, and open country pleaſed him, he might fix at Dorcheſter. But if he loved meadows and woodlands, he muſt make choice of Blandford.

This town has been twice burnt almoſt within the memory of man. The laſt fire, which was in the year 1731, deſtroyed it ſo completely, that only twenty-ſix houſes remained ſtanding. Here we cannot help bemoaning the ſingular fate of theſe weſtern towns.

towns. This is the fourth of them we met with, (Dorcheſter, Crediton, and Honiton were the other three,) which have been totally, in a manner, deſtroyed by fire. To theſe might be added Wareham, and very lately Mine-head.

Near Blandford ſtands Eaſtbury, the ſeat of Lord Melcombe; but it did not much attract our curioſity; as it is more celebrated for the ſplendor of the houſe than the ſcenery around it.

Brianſton, Mr. Portman's ſeat, which is near the town, I ſuppoſe, is a much more pleaſing place. We were not at his houſe; but ſaw enough of his woody hill, and the variety both of its ſteep and eaſy ſlopes, together with the vale and winding river, over which it hangs, to regret the cloſing in of the evening upon us, before we had finiſhed our walk.

From Blandford the country ſtill continues wild and uncultivated, yet full of antiquities; among which the moſt celebrated is the found-

ation

ation of a fort, called *Badbury-ring*. It makes
a confiderable figure, as we rode paft; and
feems from its elevation, its dimenfions, and
complicated works (for it has been fortified
with a triple ditch) to have been a place of uncommon ftrength.

Some parts of thefe downs are very picturefque. They are finely fpread, and form elegant fweeps, with many pleafant views into a
woody country, which ftretches away to the
right. They poffefs indeed all the variety
taken notice of by the poet, when he fpeaks
of the

——— pure Dorfetian downs
In boundlefs profpect fpread ; here fhagged with woods,
There rich with harvefts, and there white with flocks.

In the laft epithet he is rather unhappy ; for
the fheep, which graze thefe plains, are fo far
from being *white*, that they are univerfally
wafhed all over with *red-ocre*, which greatly
injures both the paftoral and picturefque idea.

Winborn was our next ftage from Blandford ; appearing, as we approach it, to ftand
in a wild vale furrounded with wood. This
town takes its name from one of the moft celebrated

lebrated abbies of Saxon times. Its form dates
its antiquity. The great church, which is the
only part remaining, is of the heavieft and
earlieft fpecies of Saxon architecture. If it
have no beauty, however, it hath at leaft the
peculiarity of two contiguous and fimilar
towers ; on one of which ftood once a fpire,
equal in height, it is faid, to that of Salifbury.

In this church refts a large collection of
royal and noble bones ; but the tomb moft vifited is that of King Ethelred, (brother to Alfred the Great,) an excellent prince, juft fhewn
to his fubjects. In his early youth he engaged
in all the toils and perplexities of government.
The times were adverfe. His country was over-
run by the Danes. He encountered them in battle, and was mortally wounded. His remains
were depofited in the chancel of this church,
where the infcription upon his grave-ftone,
one fhould fuppofe, hath been occafionally repaired, or it could never have endured the
changes of fo many hundred years. His effi-
gies too, in fculptured brafs, though of miferable
workmanfhip, is, however, better than we can
fuppofe the times of Alfred could produce. In
a life fo fhort there was little to record, but the
laft great fcene of it.

U 3   S: ETHEL.

S: ETHELREDI, REGIS WEST SAX-
ONUM, MARTYRIS, QUI ANNO DOMI-
NI DCCCLXXII, XXIII APRILIS, PER
MANUS DANORUM PAGANORUM, OC-
CUBUIT.

The whole monument has a monkiſh air, and
was probably the production of later times
than thoſe of Alfred. Mr. Gough, in his ſplendid publication on ſepulchral antiquities, ſuppoſes from the form of the letters, that this inſcription is not older than the times of the Reformation, which is perhaps bringing it as
much too low, as other people are inclined to
carry it too high.

From Winborn we paſſed through a heathy,
barren, flat, unpleaſant country to Pool, which
lies about nine miles farther. This country,
unpleaſant as it is, is rendered more ſo as we
approach the town. The whole coaſt is
oozy, and when the tide ebbs, it has the appearance of a vaſt ſwamp, with which the
heathy flat before us unites in one level ſurface. Nothing, under the idea of landſcape,
can be more diſagreeable. When the tide
flows, the view is ſomewhat mended. The

water

water covering the fwamp gives fome variety
to the furface of a dead uninterefting flat.

Beyond the water appear the high lands of
the ifle of Purbeck, as it is called; though it
is, in fact, only a vaft promontory running
eight or nine miles in the form of a peninfula
along the coaft. It is wafhed by the river
Frome on one fide, and by the fea on the
other. Here are dug great quantities of that
hard fpecies of ftone, which takes the name of
the country, and is of fuch excellent ufe in
paving. Here too are found marbles more
beautiful than the marbles of Italy; but lefs
valued, becaufe more common. They are
fomething like the marbles we admired at Plymouth*; but I think more variegated. The
veins, running on a brown ground, are white,
red, and blue.

Seated high on one of the eminences of
Purbeck, far to the weft, we faw Corff-caftle;
but the diftance was too great to diftinguifh
its features clearly. The ruins of it are faid to
be the moft confiderable of the kind in England. It was reduced to this ftate by the parliament at the conclufion of the civil wars.

* See page 203.

Vaft

Vaſt piles of ruin were thrown down into the ditch; but the immenſe maſſineſs of them, and the tenacity of the mortar, will long preferve them from any farther ſeparation. The principal facts commemorated in this celebrated caſtle, are the murder of Edward the Martyr, by Elfrida; the impriſonment of Edward the Second, till he was carried to his laſt horrid confinement at Berkly-caſtle; and the long ſiege it underwent in the civil wars of Charles I. defended by Lady Banks (wife of Lord Chief Juſtice Banks, to whom it belonged) with a garriſon only of forty men, againſt an army with artillery.

In the king's library in the Britiſh Muſeum*, are a ſet of maps of the ſeveral counties of England, which belonged to the old Lord Burleigh; and are rendered curious by ſeveral of his notes and memoranda written upon their margins. To the iſland of Purbeck he ſeems to have paid great attention. His notes upon it probably have a reference to the Spaniſh invaſion. We are not to expect any picturesque remarks from Lord Burleigh: but his obſervations give us *an idea of the coaſt.* " At Stud-

* No. 18. D. III.

" land-

" land-bay he obferves that forty boats may
" land, but not without danger. At Swanage,
" boats may land, and retreat at any time of
" the tide. In this bay and Studland-bay, fix
" or feven hundred fhips, of a thoufand ton
" burden, may ride fafe in any wind. Along
" this coaft, for three miles, there is a good
" landing. Shipman's-pool is a creek, where
" the enemy cannot land more than two or
" three boats. Batterage-bay is full of rocks
" and fhelves. Such alfo are Worbarrow-bay,
" Areftmifs, and Lullworth-cove. But in
" Worbarrow-bay, and Shipman's-pool, five
" hundred fail of large fhips may ride in al-
" moft every wind."

Pool lies on a bay of the fea, which is very
intricate. The body of it is a large and commodious harbour ; but it runs into many little
creeks and winding channels, which give it the
air of a water-labyrinth. When the tide flows,
the town appears encircled with water, and
looks like Venice. But the fhores are fo low,
efpecially about Brown-ifland, (which appears
only like a bank,) that there is little picturefque
fcenery about the place. In fome parts, when
the tide is full, and you can get a few trees
into the view, you have a tolerable Dutch
land-

landfcape. In general, however, all is bare;
and that painter only, who can fkilfully fill his
foreground with figures, and marine appendages, can make a picture of it. But few painters have the art of touching fmall figures in
landfcape; though many have the misfortune
to fpoil their pictures by attempting it. The
general proportions even of fmall figures, and
their graceful actions, (for there is a fpecies of
picturefque grace, of which even *clowns* fhould
participate,) are very hard to hit. We judge
of the difficulty from the few who have excelled. Scot, who underftood the form of a
fhip, and in his fea-views could give his fkies
and water, not indeed the brilliancy of Vanderveld, yet a clearnefs, which every one could
not attain, was very deficient in the neceffary
addition of figures. He could not place their
heads on their fhoulders, nor hang on their
arms, nor fet them on their legs, nor give them
an eafy action. And yet a few touches will
do all this—it is furprifing how few—when
thofe touches are well underftood. Vanderveld could do it: Zeeman could do it; and
yet, perhaps, neither of thefe mafters underftood the anatomy of the human body. Neither of them, perhaps, could have drawn either
a leg

a leg or an arm with accuracy. But in drawing a fmall figure for a landfcape, accuracy is
not required; it is enough to underftand its *general proportion*, the *fymmetry of its parts*, and
the *effect of action*. To underftand the *effect of
action* is fo exceedingly neceffary, that nothing
hurts the eye more, than to fee a figure awkwardly ufing its arms and legs. Almoft any
eye can fee the impropriety. In the management of fmall figures, I mentioned Callot (two
of whofe pictures we had feen at Longford-
caftle) among the moft able mafters *. They
who have not an opportunity of feeing his
pictures, which are fcarce, may obferve the
fame fkill in his prints; and yet I fhould not
care to mention this mafter as a perfect model;
becaufe, with all his excellence, there is often a
degree of affectation in his attitudes. If his
figures had been large, the eye would have
taken quick difguft; but in a miniature, the ex-
aggeration of pofture is lefs ftriking.

Our route from Pool to Chrift-church led us
over a heath, wilder almoft than any we had

* See page 73.

yet

yet found; but it fcarcely lafted four miles. It ended in agreeable lanes, through country not unpleafant. At leaft the force of contraft with the country we had juft feen, gave it a pleafant appearance. Here, whenever we had an opening on the right, we had views of the fea, the Ifle of Wight, and the Needles.

From Chrift-church we proceeded to Lymington, fkirting the borders of New Foreft. But as I have given an account of this country in another work*, I fhall pafs it over here.

* See Foreft Scenery.

S E C T. XXXIII.

A T Lymington we embarked for the Iſle of Wight, and ſtood for Cowes. As we approached it, the ſhore ſoon began to form into two points of land; the nearer of which is defended by a ſmall caſtle; the farther ſeemed high ground, and woody.

As we drew nearer, the bay began to open; and as we turned the caſtle-point, an ample road, well ſecured, lay before us full of large ſhipping. The town of Cowes occupied the two ſides of the hill on the right and left. The harbour is a creek, running a conſiderable way into the country. It is formed by the river Medina, which comes down from the higher grounds, where the iſland ſwells into its greateſt breadth, and is navigable as far as Newport, about ſix miles from the ſea.

At Cowes we landed, intending to ſpend two or three days in the iſland, which we hoped would allow us ſufficient time to examine its picqureſque beauties.

The

The form of the Ifle of Wight is that of an irregular lozenge. From the eaftern point to the weftern, it ranges about twenty-three miles; from the northern to the fouthern about thirteen. Through the middle of it, in the longer direction, runs a track of high land, in fome parts rather mountainous, but of the fmooth downy kind, fit for the pafturage of fheep. From thefe high grounds we have every where a view of the ifland, and its boundaries, of the fea towards the fouth, and towards the north of the coaft of Hampfhire, from which the ifland is feparated by a channel about five or fix miles in breadth.

The fhores of the ifland on the northern fide fall almoft every where to the water in eafy declivities ; except juft at the weftern, or Needle point, where they are broken and precipitous. But all the *back of the ifland*, (as the fouthern coaft is commonly called,) which is wafhed by the tides of the ocean, is worn bare to the naked rock, and is in moft places bounded againft the fea by fteep cliffs. What depredation the waves, in a courfe of years, have made upon it, is evident from the fragments of rock which have tumbled from the undermined cliffs, and lie fcattered along the fhore.

fhore. Many of them are far out at fea; and at low water only, fhew their heads above the waves. No part of the Britifh coaft is more dangerous to veffels ungoverned, and driving in the ftorm.

From Cowes our road led us firft to Newport, along the courfe of the Medina; which afforded many happy fituations to thofe who are fortunate enough to have any of its more pleafing reaches within the view of their houfes. A tide river has always its difadvantages; but it has its advantages alfo. It is generally once or twice a day adorned with the white fails of little fkiffs paffing to and fro; and at all times with boats or anchoring-barks, which have loft the tide, and wait for its return. Thefe are picturefque circumftances, which an inland river cannot have.

Newport is the capital town in the ifland. It grew into repute from its fituation on the Medina, after Carifbroke, the natural capital, was deferted. It is a large handfome town; and its market is often a curiofity. As the ifland is fo fertile, that it is fuppofed to produce feven or eight times more grain than

its

its inhabitants confume, the overplus is commonly brought to Newport to be fhipped off, and an hundred laden waggons may fometimes be feen ranged in double lines along the market-place. The free-fchool alfo, which is a handfome room, about fifty feet long, is worth looking into, as it received greater honour than perhaps any fchool-room ever did before. When the commiffioners from the Parliament treated with King Charles I. in the Ifle of Wight, this room was chofen for the conference.

From Newport we propofed to take a view of the northern coaft, which extends from Cowes-point to St. Helen's, and is thought to contain the moft beautiful part of the ifland. This might be done in two ways; either by riding along the coaft, and feeing each *particular* place that was pointed out as moft beautiful; or by keeping along the higher grounds, and taking a *general* view of the whole together. As we could not do both, we chofe the latter, and foon found we had made the more judicious choice: for the ground quickly narrows in that part of the ifland; and we obtained

tained a good idea of its *general scenery*. Mr. Grofe's houfe at the Priory, and two or three other places, we could have wifhed to have examined more particularly; but as we fhould have been confined within hedges, we could have feen little *befides the places we imme-diately vifited.* Of the *general appearance* of the landfcape, on this fide of the ifland, fome account fhall be given at the conclufion of our circuit round it.

Part of the high grounds, over which we paffed, is called Afhy-down. On the loftieft fummit of this ridge is placed a fea-mark. When fhips are driven by the ftorm fo near the fouthern coaft of the ifland, as to lofe fight of this mark of fecurity, little hope of fafety remains. It is hardly poffible for them to avoid the rocks.

As the high grounds began to decline, we verged towards the fouthern part of the ifland, with an intention to take a view of its rocky boundaries. But we had not here the advantageous point of view, which we had on the other fide. The rocky fhores, which we wifhed to examine, can be feen no where properly, but from the fea. We could only, therefore, get a view of them from fome particular ftands,

x   which

which commanded a lengthened reach of the coaſt; and ſuch ſtands occurred but ſeldom.

From the high grounds we deſcended firſt to Sandown-bay, which lies on the ſouth coaſt, and is the only part on this ſide, where it is ſuppoſed an enemy could effect a landing. It is defended by a fort, which takes its name from the bay. But the rocks ſoon commence, and continue the guardians of the coaſt, in an almoſt uninterrupted chain from this place to the very weſtern point of the iſland.

Among the curious parts of this rocky ſcenery, we were carried to *Shanklin-chine*, a vaſt chaſm winding between two high promontories, more than a mile into the country. The chaſm opens to the ſea, upon a bed of pebbles; where generally a boat or two lie moored; and the fiſherman's hut ſtands half way up the precipice. Both ſides of the chaſm are adorned with rock, and both with wood; and it is in general a picturesque ſcene: but it has not the beauty of the dells of a mountainous country, where the wood is commonly finer, and the rocks more adorned, and more majeſtic; and where a ſtream, pouring over ledges of rock,

or

or falling down a cafcade, adds the melody of found, to the beauty of the fcene.

Near Shanklin-chine, Mr. Stanley built a cottage among the rocks, where he enjoyed the fea-breezes in the heat of fummer. It is called *Undercliff*, as it is built on a ledge of rock between the upper-cliffs and the fea. The view in front is not unpleafing. It is a fort of wild rocky valley, about half a quarter of a mile acrofs, hanging over the fea, which appears abruptly beyond it, without the intervention of any middle ground. It exhibits generally a moving picture, prefenting the track which fhips, coafting the ifland, commonly take.

As it is a *bird's-eye* view, many of thefe veffels, efpecially of the fmaller fize, appear with their mafts and fails confiderably *below the horizon*. I mention this circumftance, becaufe in a picture fuch reprefentations are rather unpleafing. In reprefenting a view of this kind, therefore, the painter (if under a neceffity to paint it) fhould always wifh to remove the veffels he introduces fo far into diftance, as to raife their mafts above the hori-

X 2

zon.

zon *. The larger the veffel is, the nearer of course fhe may approach the eye. In the *variety and motion of natural views*, we are not fo much hurt with thefe circumftances, which have a bad effect in painting; and yet a *bird's-eye* view *on water*, is always lefs pleafing than *on land*; as the variety of ground is more amufing in itfelf than water, and as it carries off the perfpective better. The *grandeur*, which an *extenfive view of the ocean* prefents, is a different idea: we are fpeaking here only of its *beauty*. If we reftrict the mafts of fhips, however, from appearing *below the horizon*, we object not to boats and birds in that fituation. The boat either fifhing or in motion, the wheeling gull, or the lengthened file of fea-fowl, appear often to great advantage *againft the bofom of the fea*; and being marked with a few ftrong touches, contribute to throw the ocean into perfpective.

But though the *fituation* of *Undercliff* or *Steephill* is pleafing, we could not fay much for what is called the *cottage*. It is covered indeed with thatch; but that makes it no more a cot-

* See this fubject treated more at large in the Foreft Scenery, vol. ii. p. 115.

tage,

tage, than ruffles would make a clown a gentleman, or a meally hat would turn a laced beau
into a miller.   We every where fee the appendages of junket and good living.   Who would
expect to find a fountain bubbling up under the
windows of a *cottage*, into an elegant carved
fhell to cool wine? The thing is beautiful; but
out of place.   The imagination does not like
to be jolted in its fenfations from one idea to
another; but to go on quietly in the fame
track, either of *grandeur* or *fimplicity*.   Eafy
contrafts it approves; but violent interruptions
it diflikes.

Pleafing ideas, no doubt, may be executed
under the form of a cottage; but to make them
pleafing, they fhould be *harmonious*.   We fometimes fee the *cottage idea* carried fo far, as to
pafte ballads on the walls with good effect.
But we need not reftrict what may be called
the *artificial cottage* to fo very clofe an imitation of the *natural one*.   In the *infide* certainly it may admit much greater neatnefs and
convenience; though even here every ornament that approaches *fplendor*, fhould be re-
jected.   Without too, though the roof be
thatched, we may allow it to cover two ftories;

X 3   and

and if it project fomewhat over the walls, the effect may be better. We fhould not object to fafhed windows; but they muft not be large; and if you wifh for a veftibule, a common brick porch, with a plain neat roof, is all we allow. We often fee the front of a cottage covered with what is called *rough caft*; which has a good effect; and this may be tinted with a yellowifh tinge mixed with lime, which is more pleafing than the cold raw tint of lime and afhes. But if in the front there is any ftonework, under the denomination of frize, archetrave, or ornament of any kind, it is too much.

The ground about a cottage fhould be neat, but artlefs. There is no occafion to plant cabbages in the front. The garden may be removed out of fight; but the lawn that comes up to the door, fhould be grazed, rather than mown. The funk-fence, the net, and the painted rail, are ideas alien to the cottage. The broad gravel walk too we totally reject; and in its room wifh only for a fimple unaffected one.

Thefe things being confidered, it may, perhaps, be a more difficult thing to rear a cottage,

with

with all its proper uniformities, than is commonly imagined; inafmuch as it may be eafier to introduce the elegances of art, than to catch the pure fimplicity of nature.

From Steephill we vifited a fcene of a very different kind, Sir Richard Worfley's feat at Appuldercomb. Here every thing was *uniformly grand.* The houfe is magnificent, and it is magnificently furnifhed. Enriched ceilings, a few good pictures, coftly hangings, fhewy carpets, Gobelin chairs, and large pier-glaffes, all correfpond; and yet not in any expenfive profufion *.

The grounds too, which were more the objects of our curiofity, are laid out in a ftile of greatnefs equal to the manfion. A woody fcene rifing behind, is a beautiful back-ground to the houfe, as well as an excellent fhelter from the north. In front is fpread a magnificent lawn, or rather a park, (for it is furnifhed with deer,) well varied, and not ill-planted, ftretching far and wide. Its boundary, in one

* Since this has been written, I am told, the houfe is adorned with fome curious pieces of Greek antiquities.

X 4   part,

part, is confined, at the diſtance of about two miles, by a hill running out like a promontory; whoſe continuous horizontal ridge might hurt the eye, if it were not crowned with a caſtle. This objeɗt ſeems well executed, and is certainly well placed. Views of the ſea, and various parts of the iſland, are judiciouſly opened from all the higher grounds about the houſe.

S E C T. XXXIV.

FROM this scene of magnificence in splendor, we visited another of magnificence in ruin. This was Carisbroke-castle, an object perhaps the best worth seeing of any in the island. Instead of passing on therefore to the Needle-cliffs, which remained yet unseen, we returned to Newport, which lies within a short walk of the castle.

Carisbroke-castle stands on elevated ground, nearly in the centre of the island. It is a fortress of great antiquity. Its towers and battlements have been the care of several princes through a long series of years; and we easily mark the style of different ages, not only from the dates, and arms, which are placed in various parts of the castle, but also in the mode of building. Its latest works have the air of modern fortification. They are constructed of earth, faced with stone, and are carried round the castle as an outwork; forming a circumference of about a mile and a half. What is properly called the castle, stands on somewhat

less

lefs than two acres of land. It is difficult on the fpot to *comprehend* the various parts of this complicated fortrefs; to *defcribe* it would be impoffible. Some of the more remarkable parts are commonly fhewn. We were carried to fee Montjoy's tower; the walls of which are eighteen feet thick. We were conducted alfo to the top of the Keep; from whence we difcovered the fea in the three directions of north, fouth, and eaft. On the weft, a hill intercepted it. We were fhewn alfo a well as curious for its *depth*, as the Keep is for its *height*; and were defired to liften to the echoes and *lengthened found*, which even a pin makes when thrown into it. There lived lately an appendage to this well, which deferved notice alfo. It was an afs, which had drawn water patiently from it, through the fpace of forty years.

Carifbroke-caftle was once the refidence of the princes of the country; and afterwards of appointed governors, when the ifland became annexed to the crown. As the inhabitants had not that ready accefs to juftice, which other parts of· the kingdom had, they fometimes fmarted under the defpotic power of their governors. Remonftrances were often made to
the

the crown; but it feems to have been a maxim of ftate, efpecially during the reign of the Tudors, to ftrengthen, rather than abridge the. power of governors in the remoter provinces; and though it was not always a maxim of juftice, it was probably a maxim of good policy. On the borders of Scotland we have many inftances of this delegated tyranny.

But though the governors of the ifland were fometimes apt to over-rule law themfelves; they were careful not to let the inhabitants feel vexations of any law, but their own. For this reafon they would never fuffer an attorney to fettle in the ifland. In the Oglander family are preferved fome memoirs of the country, written by Sir John Oglander, one of their anceftors, in which we are told, that in the reign of Elizabeth, when Sir George Cary was governor of the ifland, an attorney came fneaking into it, with a view to fettle. Sir George hearing of him had him apprehended; and ordering bells to be faftened about his legs, and a lighted firebrand tied to his back, he turned him loofe to the populace, who hunted him out of the ifland *.

* See Sir R. Worfley's Account of the Ifle of Wight.

Adjoining

Adjoining to Carifbroke-caftle is a royal domain, called Parkhurft, or Carifbroke-foreft. It contains about three thoufand acres; and muft have been, when its woods were luxuriant, very beautiful. It is now a naked fcene; but we faw its elegant lines with more advantage, than if it had been adorned with all its fylvan drapery. The deer, its ancient inhabitants, are now nearly extinct; and it is grazed by fheep, and little groups of wild horfes, which are not lefs ornamental.

The great hiftorical circumftance of Carifbroke-caftle, is its having been long the prifon of diftreffed majefty. Many a mournful tale on this fubject, the noble hiftorian of thofe times hath told us. He is circumftantial in his relation of the unhappy Charles's imprifonment here. But in an account of the Ifle of Wight, collected by an anceftor of the Worfley-family, and printed, though in few hands, fome circumftances with regard to that event are mentioned, which had not come to the ears of Lord Clarendon.

That hiftorian tells us, through what means this unfortunate prince threw himfelf into the power of Colonel Hammond, who was then governor of the Ifle of Wight. Hammond,

mond, however, feems to have been a man of humanity; and while his hands were untied, was difpofed to fhew the king every civility in his power. Charles took his exercife on horfe-back, where he pleafed; though his motions were probably obferved; and, as the parliament had granted him five thoufand pounds a year, he lived a few months in fomething like royal ftate.

But this liberty was foon abridged: his chaplains and fervants were firft taken from him; then his going abroad in the ifland gave offence; and foon after, his intercourfe with any body, but thofe fet about him. So foli-tary were his hours, during a great part of his confinement, that as he was one day ftanding near the gate of the caftle, with Sir Philip Warwick, he pointed to an old decrepid man walking acrofs one of the courts, and faid, that man is fent every morning to light my fire; and is the beft companion I have had for many months.

All this fevere ufage Charles bore with pa-tience and equanimity, and endeavoured as much as poffible to keep his mind employed. He had ever been imprefled with ferious thoughts of religion, which his misfortunes had

now

now ſtrengthened and confirmed. Devotion, meditation, and reading the ſcriptures, were his great conſolation. The few books he had brought with him into the caſtle, were chiefly on religious ſubjects; or of a ſerious caſt. Among them was Hooker's Eccleſiaſtical Polity. This book, it is probable, he had ſtudied with great attention; as it related much to the national queſtions of that time, in which no man was better verſed. In his ſlender catalogue we find alſo two books of amuſement, Taſſo's Jeruſalem, and Spencer's Fairy Queen. If Charles had *acted* with as much judgment as he *read*, and had ſhewn as much *diſcernment in life*, as he had *taſte in the arts*, he might have figured among the greateſt princes. Every lover of pictureſque beauty, however, muſt reſpect this amiable prince, notwithſtanding his political weakneſſes. We never had a prince in England, whoſe genius and taſte were more elevated and exact. He ſaw the arts in a very enlarged point of view. The amuſements of his court were a model of elegance to all Europe; and his cabinets were the receptacles only of what was exquiſite in ſculpture and painting. None but men of the firſt merit in their profeſſion found encouragement from

him;

him; and thefe abundantly. Jones was his architect, and Vandyck his painter. Charles was a fcholar, a man of tafte, a gentleman, and a chriftian; he was every thing but a king. The *art of reigning* was the *only art* of which he was ignorant.

But though a love for the arts, we fee, has no connection with *political wifdom*; yet we cannot fo eafily give up its tendency to *meliorate the heart*. This effect we may *prefume at leaft* it had on Charles.

To this fuppofition in favor of the arts, it is objected, that we often fee among profeffional men very abandoned libertines. But I fhould here wifh to fuggeft a diftinction between an *innate love for what is beautiful*, and that fort of *mechanical turn*, which can happily delineate, colour, and exprefs, an object of beauty. The one is feated in the *heart*, and the other in the *eye and in the fingers*. The *mechanical man*, merely following his profeffion, is governed by no idea, but that of enriching himfelf. It is not the love of beauty with which he is fmitten, but the love of money. He paints a picture with as little enthufiafm, as a blackfmith fhoes a horfe. All this is fordid. Whereas the true admirer of art feels his mind thoroughly impreffed

impreffed with the *love of beauty.* He is tranfported with it in nature; and he admires it in
art, the fubftitute of nature. The love of
beauty may exift without a hand to execute
the images it excites. It may exift the more
ftrongly perhaps for being only *felt*; for the
conceptions of genius never rife in value from
their being embodied. The *embodied form* is
always below the *original idea.*

The beauteous forms of nature and art thus
impreffed on the mind, give it a difpofition to
happinefs, from the habit of being pleafed, from
the habit of feeking always for pleafing objects,
and making even difpleafing objects agreeable
by throwing on them fuch colours of imagination, as improve their defects; and if a *love
for beauty* is not immediately connected with
moral ideas, we may at leaft fuppofe that it
foftens the mind, and puts it in a frame to
receive them. " An intimate acquaintance
" with the works of art and genius, in their
" moft beautiful and amiable forms, (fays an
" agreeable writer,) harmonizes and fweetens
" the temper, opens and extends the imagin-
" ation, and difpofes to the moft pleafing
" views of mankind and Providence. By con-
" fidering nature in this favourable point of
3   " view,

" view, the heart is dilated, and filled with
" the moſt benevolent ſentiments : and then
" indeed the ſecret ſympathy and connection
" between the feelings of natural and moral
" beauty, the connection between a good taſte
" and a good heart, appears with the greateſt
" luſtre *."

We left the unhappy Charles, who occa-
ſioned theſe remarks, in one of the gloomy
manſions of Cariſbroke-caſtle, amuſing his ſo-
litary hours with Hooker's Eccleſiaſtical Polity,
and Spencer's Fairy Queen. His exerciſe was
now much abridged. He was ſkilled in horſe-
manſhip, and fond of riding. But as this was
refuſed, he ſpent two or three hours every
morning in walking on the ramparts of the
caſtle. Here he enjoyed at leaſt a fine air, and
an extenſive proſpect ; though every object he
ſaw, the flocks ſtraying careleſsly on one ſide,
and the ſhips ſailing freely on the other, put
him in mind of that liberty, of which he was
ſo cruelly deprived.

In the mean time, he was totally careleſs of
his perſon. He let his beard and his hair
grow, and was inattentive to his dreſs. " They

---

* Gregory's Compar. View, p. 236.

Y   " who

" who had feen him," (fays Lord Clarendon)
" a year before, thought his countenance ex-
" tremely altered; his hair was grey, and his
" appearance very different from what it had
" been."

There is a picture of him at Sion-houfe, in
which the diftreffes of his mind are ftrongly
characterifed on his countenance. A perfon
is reprefented delivering him a letter, which
may be fuppofed to contain bad news. Charles's
features were always compofed and ferious; but
here they are heightened with a melancholy
air, and yet they are marked alfo with mildnefs
and fortitude. It is a very affecting picture, as
it brings ftrongly before us the feelings of this
amiable prince, on the moft difaftrous events of
his life. It is painted fo much in the manner
of Vandyck, that it might eafily be miftaken
for one of his beft pictures. But it was certainly painted by Sir Peter Lely, who copied
after Vandyck, when he firft came into England. Vandyck died in the year 1641, which
was before the troubles of Charles began.

During the time of his imprifonment in
Carifbroke-caftle, three attempts were made,
chiefly by the gentlemen of the ifland, to ref-
cue him. Lord Clarendon gives us the detail

of

of two of them; but a third, which he had
heard of, he fuppofes to have been a mere
fiction. As it is mentioned, however, in the
Worfley papers, with every mark of authen-
ticity, and as one of the principal conductors
of it was a gentleman of that family, there
feems to be little doubt of its being a fact.
The following is an abftract of it.

By a correfpondence privately fettled with
fome gentlemen in the ifland, it was agreed,
that the king fhould let himfelf down by a cord
from a window in his apartment. A fwift
horfe, with a guide, were to wait for him at
the bottom of the ramparts; and a veffel in
the offing was to be ready to convey him
where he pleafed. The chief difficulty in the
fcheme was in the firft ftep. The affociating
gentlemen were doubtful how the king fhould
get through the iron bars of his window. But
Charles affured them, he had tried the paffage,
and did not doubt but it was fufficiently large.
All things, therefore, were now prepared, the
hour was come, and the fecret fign thrown up
to the king's window. Charles being ready,
began the attempt; but he foon found he had
made a falfe calculation. Having protruded
his head and fhoulders, he could get no farther;

ther ; and what was worfe, having made great
exertions thus far, he could not draw himfelf
back. His friends at the bottom heard him
groan in his diftrefs, but were unable to relieve
him. At length, however, by repeated efforts
he got himfelf difengaged; but made at that
time no farther attempt. Afterwards he contrived to faw the bars of his window afunder;
and another fcheme was laid; but the particulars of this, Lord Clarendon details.

The treaty at Newport foon followed; after
which Charles was feized by the army, and
carried a prifoner to Hurft-caftle. In his way
thither he met Mr. Worfley, one of the
gentlemen who had rifked his life for him at
Carifbroke. Charles wrung his hand with
affection, and pulling his watch out of his
pocket, gave it to him, faying, " That is all
" my gratitude has to give."

This watch is ftill preferved in the family.
It is of filver, large and clumfy in its form.
The cafe is neatly ornamented with filagree;
but the movements are of very ordinary workmanfhip, and wound up with catgut. I mention thefe particulars merely for the fake of
obferving, that the arts do not certainly troop
in companies together fo much as they are
often

often reprefented. At the time when this clumfy piece of mechanifm was made, which we may fuppofe was the work of the beft artift of his day, architecture and painting were at a height, which they have never exceeded. The cafe feems to be this; when art has a model before it, (as painting has nature, and architecture the Grecian orders,) it foon arrives at perfection. But fuch arts as depend on invention, fcience, and mechanic fkill, work their way but flowly in a country *.

From Carifbroke-caftle we propofed to vifit the weftern parts of the ifland, and took our courfe, as before, along the higher grounds, through the middle of the country. Our road led us near Swanfton, the feat of Sir Fitzwilliam Barrington, which feems to be a pleafant fcene: and afterwards near Weftover-lodge, the habitation of Mr. Holmes, where we obferved nothing very interefting.

* In the year 1793, on digging a grave in the church of Newport, a leaden coffin was found, with this infcription : ELISA-BETH, 2ᵈ DAUGHTER OF THE LATE KING CHARLES, DECEASED SEP 8ᵗʰ, MDCL.

A little

A little ftream, which we crofs here, falling
down to the northern coaft, forms at Newtown,
a few miles below, one of the beft natural har-
bours in the ifland. The ftreets and veftiges
of a confiderable town are here traced; but
fcarce a houfe is ftanding. Whether it was
planned and never built, or whether it was deftroyed and never reftored, feems to be matter
of uncertainty. It is the general opinion, that
it was burnt in fome Danifh invafion. But its
being reprefented in parliament feems rather
to indicate its having had a period of later
exiftence.

From hence we proceeded to Yarmouth,
where Henry VIII. built a caftle to defend the
entrance through the Needles, between the Ifle
of Wight and the coaft of Hampfhire; on which
coaft ftands Hurft, another caftle oppofite to
that at Yarmouth.

Here the ifland draws nearly to a point.
The extreme part of it is almoft feparated from
the main body by a creek, which runs up from
Yarmouth almoft to the oppofite fhore. The
narrow ifthmus is called Frefhwater-gate. Here
we

we found ourfelves among rocks and precipices
of wonderful height, and had from this ftand a
view of an extended range of chalky cliffs,
running along the fouthern coaft of the ifland.
Here too we found a perforated cave; which
in fome pofitions makes a picturefque foreground, while the fea appearing through it,
has a good effect.

SECT. XXXV.

WE had now taken a view of the ifland from one end to the other, and on the whole, found ourfelves rather difappointed in the chief objeſt of our purfuit, which was the picturefque beauty of its fcenery.

Picturefque beauty is a phrafe but little underſtood. We precifely mean by it that kind of beauty which *would look well in a piſture*. Neither grounds laid out by art, nor improved by agriculture, are of this kind. The Ifle of Wight is, in faſt, a large garden, or rather a field, which in every part has been disfigured by the fpade, the coulter, and the harrow. It abounds much more in tillage than in pafturage; and of all fpecies of cultivation, cornlands are the moſt unpiſturefque. The regularity of corn-fields difgufts; and the colour of corn, efpecially near harveſt, is out of tune with every thing elfe.

Yet thefe *manufaſtured fcenes* are commonly thought to be *piſturefque*. You rarely meet a defcription of the beauties of the country, in which

which fome of its *artificial appendages* do not
make a part of the landfcape. And in *poetry*
all thefe circumftances appear with advantage :

> Sometimes walking, not unfeen,
> By hedge-row elms, on hillocks green :
> While the plowman, near at hand,
> Whiftles o'er the furrowed land;
> And the milk-maid finging blithe ;
> And the mower whets his fcithe.

But however pleafing all this may be in poetry,
on canvafs, hedge-row elms, furrowed lands,
meadows adorned with milk-maids, and hay-
fields adorned with mowers, have a bad effect.

In confidering the Ifle of Wight in a picturefque light, we divide it into three kinds of
landfcape, the *high grounds*, the *lower cultivated parts*, and the *rocky fcenes*.

The *high grounds*, which, as we juft obferved,
run from the eaftern to the weftern point,
through the middle of the ifland, are the only
parts of the country which are in a ftate of nature ; and yet even thefe are not wholly fo:
for large farms have, in many parts, made in-
croachments upon them, and cut them into
fquares by regular hedges, and inclofed fheep-
walks. Sometimes, however, from thefe
heights, we are able to obtain a fweep of country,

try unincumbered with the intrufions of art. About Carifbroke-foreft particularly, for many miles together, we fee nothing like cultivation.

But ftill the beft of thefe views afford little more than what may be called *extenfive foregrounds*. Of *diftant country* we meet with nothing in a grand ftile, notwithftanding our elevation. In fome parts we find little dips from the higher grounds into woody bottoms, and in other parts diftances of a few miles in extent over the country below, but nothing that is remote enough to affume grandeur.

A diftance muft ftretch away many leagues from the eye; it muft confift of various *intermediate parts*; it muft be enriched by *numerous objects*, which lofe by degrees all form and diftinctnefs; and finally perhaps *terminate* in faint purple mountains, or perhaps mix with the blue mifts of ether, before it can pretend to the character of *grandeur*. Such were the fcenes prefented to us from the heights of Pontic, and the hills of Quantoc*. But here we had nothing of this kind. A fcanty ifland could not afford them. Sometimes indeed,

* See pages 149 and 161,

when

when the foregrounds were happily difpofed
with the fea beyond them, we got a grand and
fimple fea-view, *grander* perhaps than the diftances I have juft been alluding to, as confifting of *fewer parts*; but for that reafon lefs
beautiful and *amufing*.

The northern coaft between Cowes and St.
Helen's is generally confidered as the moft
beautiful part of the ifland; and it prefents, no
doubt, many lawns and woods, and a variety
of ground, which muft be ever pleafing: but
ftill we have only little, pleafant, paftoral
fcenes; and thefe but feldom in any perfection; for as the whole country is under the
difcipline of cultivation, the picturefque eye is
every where more or lefs offended.

To this may be added, that there is a great
deficiency of wood. Though here and there
a few plantations about improved fcenes, make
a contraft with the lawns they adorn; the
country, in general is naked; and yet even fo
late as in Charles II.'s time, there were woods
in the ifland fo complete and extenfive, that it
is faid a fquirrel might have travelled in feveral
parts, many leagues together, on the tops of
the trees. Thefe woods, however, are now
almoft univerfally cut down.

But

But it is faid, the ifland does not depend fo much on its *home fcenery*. Its views over the channel and the Hampfhire coaft are its pride. Thefe views, however, are far from being the moft beautiful of their kind, and much lefs beautiful than we had expected to find them. They want the great ingredients of a pleafing *coaft view*, a *variety of line*, and an *extent of diftance*. Either of thefe ingredients would be a foundation for beauty; but here both are wanting.

In the firft place, a *variety of line* is wanting. The line of the oppofite coaft runs generally in a ftraight unbroken courfe for many leagues. At leaft it appears to deviate fo little from a ftraight line, that the deviation is loft. Whereas the true beautiful *coaft line* breaks away in various irregular curves, forming either grand rocky projections, or ample bays fweeping from the eye in winding perfpective. Thefe ideas we had unhappily at this time ftrong in recollection, having juft left the fhores of the Briftol channel, in which they abound. The comparifon gave additional tamenefs to the lines of the Hampfhire coaft.

But

But an *extent of country* might have made fome amends for the want of *variety in the lines.* We had, however, no more of this circum-ftance than of the other. The whole length of the coaft prefents only a narrow edging of land. Whenever you hear the beauties of it mentioned, you always hear *places named*; but never a *country defcribed.* You are never told, for inftance, that the country forms fome ample vale, with wooded hills winding on each fide; or that the fcene at firft is woody, beyond which the country retires into remote diftance. Nothing of this kind you hear; for nothing of this kind exifts. Inftead of this beautiful fcenery, you are informed, you may fee Portf-mouth, and Gofport, and Lymington, and a number of other places, which lie near the fhore. And fo you may with a good glafs; for it is the cuftom of the ifland always to con-template landfcape through a telefcope.

There are indeed times when views on this coaft are grander than can be exhibited in any part of the world. When the navy of England is forming a rendezvous at Spithead, or waiting for a wind at St. Helen's, every curious per-fon, who loves a grand fight, would wifh for a ftand on the ifland-coaft. And indeed the

eaftern

eaftern end of it is generally entertained with fome exhibition of this kind, even in time of peace; for though a fleet of thirty or forty fail of the line is not continually riding near the coaft, yet generally, either fome fhips of war, or two or three frigates, are paffing or re-paffing from Portfmouth-harbour, going out on a cruife, or returning from one.

Thefe are fights with which the weftern coafts of the ifland are not often entertained. The telefcope there is feldom levelled at fleets, or fhips of the line. Sometimes a folitary frigate, with a fair wind, or an Indiaman, may lead through the Needles, and attract the atten-tion of the weftern iflanders; but on that fide of the coaft they muft generally be content with views adorned with fkiffs, paffage-boats, and fleets of whiting-fifhers. If, however, they will be content to fubftitute the *picturefque* in the room of the *grand*, they have in thefe minuter appendages the advantage of their eaftern neighbours.

Having thus confidered the *higher* and *lower* grounds of the Ifle of Wight, we confider laftly its *rocky fcenery*. This is feldom an ornament to the

the scenes of the island, as it is seldom seen from any part of it. Sometimes you may get a perspective view of a range of rocky-coast; but in general the rocks of the island make a shew only at sea * ; and there they are *grand*, rather than *picturesque*. Their *height* gives them grandeur, some of them rearing themselves six hundred feet above the level of the water. Their *extent* also is magnificent, as they range in some places perhaps a dozen miles along the coast. But their *form* and *colour* unite in injuring their beauty.

With regard to their *form*, instead of presenting those noble masses, and broad surfaces of projecting rocks, which we see along many of the coasts of England, they are broken and crumbled into minute parts. The chalky substance, of which they are constructed, has not consistence to spread into an ample surface. It shivers too much. If I were to describe these rocks therefore in two words, I should call them *magnificently little*. This, however, is a disadvantage only on the *foreground*. *At sea* all these frittered parts dissolve away, and are melted by distance into broad surfaces.

* See page 306.

But

But here again the *colour* offends. Thefe cliffs are not chalk, yet are fo like chalk, that the foffilift hardly knows what elfe to call them. The painter is in the fame dilemma. He finds them not white, but fo nearly white, that he hardly knows what other colour to give them. Nature has, in many parts, fpread over them a few ftains and tints, as fhe feems always ftudious to remove an offenfive glare. But on fo large a furface, this has but a partial effect; and the whole coaft, for many leagues together, appears nearly white. Now of all hues the painter diflikes white the moft; as it is the moft refractory and unaccommodating to his other tints. Of courfe, therefore, the cliffs of the Ifle of Wight offend him.

From this uniformity of colour, the rocks of Allum-bay fhould be excepted; the ftrata of which are tinted, and marbled with red, brown, blue, and other colours, in a beautiful manner. This bay is nearly oppofite to Hurft-caftle, and is the moft weftern inlet, which is formed on the northern fide of the ifland.

There is one circumftance belonging to the weftern rocks of the Ifle of Wight, which, though

though but a trifling one, is of a picturesque nature, and ought, therefore, to be mentioned. At periodical seasons, they are frequented with prodigious flights of sea-fowl of various kinds. Their numbers can only be described by the hyperbolical expression of *darkening the air.* They sit commonly, when they are not in motion, on the ledges of the cliffs; in the crannies of which they breed. You see them ranged in black files through a confiderable space. The report of a gun brings them all out of their receffes; and the air, which a moment before was still and quiet, is now beaten with myriads of busy wings, and filled with screams and cries as various as the several tribes from which they iffue. " We have often refted on " our oars under the rocks," (says Mr. Pennant, with much defcriptive elegance,) " attentive to " the founds above our heads, which, mixed " with the folemn roar of the waves fwelling " into the vaft caverns beneath, and retiring " from them, produced a fine effect. The fharp " note of the fea-gull, the loud fcream of the " awk, together with the hoarfe, deep, peri- " odical croak of the cormorant, which ferves " as a bafe to the reft, often furnifhed us with

z " a con-

" a concert, and, joined with the wild fcenery
" that furrounded us, afforded us a high degree
" of pleafure." But it is not, I think, from
novelty, to which Mr. Pennant afcribes it, that
the pleafure arifes. Thefe notes, though dif-
cordant in themfelves, are in perfect harmony
with the wild fcenes where they are heard;
and this makes them chiefly interefting. In
the views, therefore, of this rocky coaft, thefe
flights of birds fhould never be forgotten, as
they may well be numbered among its picturefque appendages.

Neither fifh nor fowl can haunt a coaft, but
the inhabitants find fome means of turning
them to advantage. Thefe airy inmates of fuch
cliffs and precipices as hang beetling many fathoms above the fea, one fhould imagine might
pafs their lives in full fecurity. But man, with
the hand of art, contrives to reach them. He
fixes an iron crow firm in the ground, and
tying a rope tight to it, he lets himfelf down
with a bafket in his hand, among the middle
regions of the cliffs, where the fowls inhabit.
So bold and fudden an invafion frights them
immediately from their receffes. With a watch-
ful eye he examines the parts of the rock
from

from which they chiefly efcape; and fcrambling about by the help of his rope, he fills his bafket with their eggs, for which he can always find a ready market.

Thefe birds alfo furnifh *amufement* to all the neighbouring country. In fummer, a number of fhooting parties are formed both by land and fea; and when the weather is fine, you can feldom fail paft without falling in with fome of them.

That man has a right to deftroy fuch animals as are *noxious* to him is undoubted. That he has a right alfo over the lives of fuch animals as are *ufeful* to him for food and other neceffaries, is equally unqueftioned. But whether he has a right to deftroy life for his *amufement*, is another queftion. If he is determined to *act the tyrant*, (that is, to confider *power* as conferring *right*,) the point is decided. Power he certainly has. But if he wifh to act on authorized and equitable principles, let him juft point out the paffage in his charter of rights over the brute creation, which gives him the liberty of deftroying life for his *amufement* *.

I fhall

* On Noah, and in him on all mankind,
The charter was conferred, by which we hold

The

I fhall conclude thefe remarks on the numerous flights of fea-fowl, with a paffage from
Vaillent's Travels in Africa, which is the moft
curious of the kind I have met with. On his
landing on Daffen ifland, at the mouth of
Saldanha-bay, near the cape of Good Hope,
he tells us, " there rofe fuddenly from the
" whole furface of the ifland an immenfe ca-
" nopy, or rather a fky, compofed of birds of
" every fpecies and of all colours, cormorants,
" fea-gulls, fea-fwallows, pelicans, &c. I believe
" all the winged tribe of Africa were here affem-
" bled. All their voices united together, formed
" fuch horrid mufic, that I was every moment
" obliged to cover my head to give a little

The flefh of animals in fee ; and claim
O'er all we feed on, power of life and death.
But read the inftrument, and mark it well.
The oppreffion of a tyrannous control
Can find no warrant there.
    I would not enter on my lift of friends
(Though graced with polifhed manners and fine fenfe,
Yet wanting fenfibility) the man
Who needlefsly fets foot upon a worm.
    The fum is this. If man's convenience, health,
Or fafety interfere, his rights and claims
Are paramount, and muft extinguifh theirs.
Elfe they are all—the meaneft things that are—
As free to live, and to enjoy that life,
As God was free to form them at the firft,
Who in his fovereign wifdom made them all.

                                                       " relief

" relief to my ears. The alarm which we
" fpread was the more general among thefe
" legions of birds, as we principally difturbed
" the females who were then fitting. They
" had nefts, eggs, and young to defend. They
" were like furious harpies let loofe againft us.
" They often flew fo near us, that they flap-
" ped their wings in our faces; and though
" we fired repeatedly, we could not frighten
" them. It feemed almoft impoffible to dif-
" perfe the cloud. We could not move a ftep
" without crufhing either eggs or young ones.
" The earth was entirely ftrewed with them."

There is, befides thefe flights of birds, another picturefque circumftance frequently feen
on the coafts of the Ifle of Wight, which may
be mentioned, though it is a dreadful one,
that of fhipwrecks. As the diftreffes of mankind furnifh the choiceft fubjects for dramatic
fcenes, fo do they often for painting. And
among thefe, no marine fubject is equal to a
fhipwreck in the hands of a mafter. I put it
into the hands of a mafter, becaufe I have more
frequently feen this fubject mifmanaged than
any other. A winter feldom paffes in which

the

the inhabitants of thefe dangerous coafts are not called together to fee fome dreadful event of this kind. Long experience has taught them to judge, when the mifchief is inevitable. They fee that every wave, which beats over the perifhing veffel, drives her nearer fome reefs of rocks, well known to them, though the feaman knows it not. Signals can be of no ufe; yet they make what fignals they can to point out the danger. In a fhort moment the dreadful crafh arrives. The labouring veffel, now beating among the rocks, gives way in every part; and the hofpitable iflanders, very unlike their neighbours on the Cornifh coaft, have nothing left but to do every thing in their power to fave the miferable people, and recover what they can from the wreck.

Having now finifhed our view of the Ifle of Wight, we returned from the rocks of Frefhwater to Yarmouth, where we took boat for Lymington.

S E C T. XXXVI.

IT has long been a queſtion among natu-
 raliſts, whether the Iſle of Wight was ever
joined to the coaſt of Hampſhire? Its weſtern
point has greatly the appearance of having
been torn and convulſed. Thoſe vaſt inſulated
rocks, called the *Needles*, ſeem plainly to have
been waſhed away from the ſhores of the
iſland. One of them, which was known by
the name of *Lot's Wife*, a tall ſpiral rock, was
undermined and ſwallowed up by the ſea not
many years ago; and there is every probability that the reſt will follow.

What renders this ſeparation of the iſland
from the main ſtill more probable is, that the
ſea makes yearly depredations along that part of
the Hampſhire coaſt called *Hordle-cliff*, which
is juſt oppoſite to the Needles. It has been
obſerved too, that there are chalk-rocks at the
bottom of the water, exactly like the Needles,
all along the channel towards Chriſtchurch.

The beſt *recorded authority* which we have
of this early union between the Iſle of Wight

and

and the main, is given us by Diodorus Siculus. This writer, fpeaking of the tin trade in Britain, informs us, that the people of Cornwall brought this metal to a certain ifland called *Ictis*, for the fake of its being more eafily tranfported from thence to the Continent; into which ifland they carried it in carts, when the tide ebbed; for *Ictis*, he fays, was only an ifland at full fea*.

By *Ictis*, it is fuppofed, Diodorus meant the Ifle of Wight; the ancient name of which was *Vectis*, a name nearly fimilar. This opinion however has been oppofed by fome; and particularly by Mr. Borlafe in his Antiquities of Cornwall, who rather fuppofes the *Ictis* of Diodorus to be fome ifland, though he does not well fettle where, upon the coaft of Cornwall. But Mr. Whitaker, in his Hiftory of Manchefter, has brought forward the old opinion again with new authority.

If then this fuppofition is at length well grounded, we may gather from it thefe points of information, that the Ifle of Wight was once a vaft promontory, running out into the fea, like the Ifle of Purbeck at this time; that

* Lib. iv. p. 301. ed. Hen.

it was then united folidly to the coaft of Hampfhire at its weftern point, and in all other parts furrounded by the fea; but that about two thoufand years ago, (which is fomewhat before the time of Diodorus,) the fea had gained fo far upon it, that it became infular and peninfular, according to the flux and reflux of the tide, till at length the fea, gaining ftill farther poffeffion, formed it, as it is at prefent, into an abfolute ifland.

As we entered Lymington-river, we found a frefh proof of the probability of the ancient union between Vectis and the main. The tide was gone, and had left vaft ftretches of ooze along the deferted fhores. Here we faw lying on the right, a huge ftump of a tree, which our boatman informed us had been dragged out of the water. He affured us alfo, that roots of oaks, and other trees, were often found on thefe banks of mud, which feems ftill to ftrengthen the opinion that all this part of the coaft, now covered with the tide, had once been foreft-land.

S E C T. XXXVII.

FROM Lymington we proceeded to Southampton ; but all this part of the country,
through New-Foreſt, as far as to the bay of
Southampton, hath been examined in another
work *.

At Redbridge we croſſed the river, which
flows into Southampton-bay, over a long
wooden bridge and cauſeway, ſometimes covered by the tide. Ships of conſiderable burden come up as far as this bridge, where they
take in timber from New-Foreſt, and other
commodities.

A little beyond Redbridge, at a place called
Milbroke, a beautiful view opens of Southampton. Before us lay Southampton-bay,
ſpreading into a noble ſurface of water. The
town runs out like a peninſula on the left, and,
with its old walls and towers, makes a piĉtu-
reſque appearance. On the right, forming the
other ſide of the bay, appear the ſkirts of New-

* Foreſt Scenery.

Foreſt,

Foreft, and the opening in front is filled with a diftant view of the Ifle of Wight.

Southampton is an elegant well-built town. It ftands on the confluence of two large wa-ters ; and when the tide is full, is feated on a peninfula.   It is a town of great antiquity, and ftill preferves its refpe&table appendages of ancient walls and gates.   The country around is beautiful.

At Southampton we took boat to fee the ruins of Netley-Abbey, which lie about three miles below on the bay.   As we approached, nothing could be feen from the water ; the bank is high and woody, and fkreens every thing beyond it.   Having landed and walked up the meadows about a quarter of a mile, we entered a circular valley, which feems to be a mile in circumference, and is fkreened with wood on every fide *, except that which opens to a part of the river, and which has probably once been wooded alfo.   In a dip, near the centre of this valley, ftands Netley-abbey.   As you approach it, you fee buildings only of the moft ordinary fpecies, gable-ends and fquare

* I believe much of this wood is now cut down.

walls,

walls, without any ornament, except a few heavy buttreffes.

You enter a large fquare, which was formerly known by the name of the Fountain-court. The fide on which you enter feems to have been once chambered, and divided into various offices. Such alfo was the left fide of the court, where the bakery and ovens may ftill be traced. But in general, whatever the rooms have been which occupied thefe two fides, the traces of them are very obfcure. On the third fide, oppofite to the entrance, the court is bounded by the fouth wall of the great church; and along the fourth fide range different apartments, which are the moft perfect of any that remain in this whole mafs of ruin.

The firft you enter feems to have been a dining-hall. It is twenty-five paces long and nine broad, and has been vaulted, and chambered above. Adjoining to it, on the right, are the pantry and kitchen. You ftill fee in the former the aperture, or buttery-hatch, through which victuals were conveyed into the hall. The kitchen of Netley-Abbey is inferior to that of Glaftonbury, but is a fpacious and lofty vaulted room; and what is peculiar, from one fide of it leads a fubterraneous paffage to the river, which fome imagine to have been a common

mon fewer, but it is too ample, I fhould fuppofe, to have been intended for that purpofe.

At the other end of the dining-hall, you
pafs through a fmall vaulted room, into the
chapter-houfe, which is ten paces fquare. This
room is beautifully proportioned, and adorned
on each fide by three arches, which uniting at
the top in ribs, fupport a vaulted roof. To
this adjoin two fmaller rooms, from whence
there is an entrance to the great church by the
crofs aifle.

The great church has been a very elegant
piece of Gothic architecture; and is almoft
the only part of the whole ruin, which is picturefque. All traces of the aifles and pillars
are loft; but the walls are entire, except half
the crofs-aifle, which is gone. The eaft and
weft windows remain; the former has not yet
loft all its ornaments; and both are very beautiful without, as well as within. Maundrel tells
us, that the eaft windows in all the Chriftian
churches he met with in his travels as far as
Tyre, which were not fewer than a hundred,
were left uninjured *. A fimilar remark, I
think, may be made on moft of the ruined
churches in England. The fact is fingular,

* Maundrel's Travels, p. 49.

3   but

but whether it is owing to chance or fuperftition may be doubted. In that part of the
crofs-aifle at Netley-Abbey which remains, a
fmall part of the ftone roof is ftill left, and is a
very curious fpecimen of Gothic antiquity.

More of this roof might ftill have remained
if the warnings of Heaven (as that renowned
antiquarian Brown Willis informs us) had
taken effect. From him we have an anecdote,
which, *he affures us*, is founded on fact, of a
carpenter, who once trafficked with the owner
of Netley for this elegant roof, which he
meant to pull down and convert into gain.
As he retired to reft, his flumbers were difturbed with dreadful dreams. Thefe having
no effect, the next night vifions appeared;
venerable old men in Monkifh habits, with
frowning faces and threatening hands. Still
he purfued his wicked purpofe. But the next
night he had fcarce fallen afleep, when a monftrous coping-ftone fell plumb upon his head.
He ftarted with horror, and was hardly at
length perfuaded it was a dream. All this
having only a momentary effect, in the morning he went to work on the execution of his
defign. No farther warning was given him.
He had fcarce mounted a ladder, when a coping-ftone fell in earneft from the roof, and put
him

him to inftant death. Others, however, it
feems, have been found, notwithftanding this
example, who have purfued the defign, for a
mere fragment of the roof only now remains.

The prefent poffeffor purfues an oppofite
extreme. The whole body of the church is
now fo choaked with ruin, and overgrown
with thickets and ivy-bufhes, that the greateft
part of the building is invifible. A degree of
all thefe, no doubt, would be ornamental ; but
like other ornaments, when they are too profufely fcattered, they offend. Thefe ruins are
as much obftructed on the outfide, as they are
within. We walked round them, and could
find only two places, the two end windows,
where we could poffibly take a view. Every
other approach is excluded, except on the fide
we entered, which leaft deferves to be expofed.
This part is fo very ordinary, that it raifes a
prejudice at firft againft the whole; and the
ruin would be fhewn to much more advantage
if this fide were blocked up with wood, and
the approach made either by the eaft or weft
window of the great church. Beyond the
ruins are the remains of large ftew-ponds,
which were formerly appendages of the
abbey.

SECT. XXXVIII.

A S we set sail from Netley-Abbey, we had a
beautiful view of Southampton, running
from us in a point directly opposite to that
view which we had from Redbridge. The
indentations made by the river Itchin, and other
creeks, are great advantages to the view.

From Southampton we took our rout to
Winchester, through a very beautiful country.
The first object is an artificial avenue, composed of detached groups of fir. The idea of an
avenue as a connecting thread between a town
and a country, is a good one. We observe,
however, that the beauty of this avenue is
much greater as we approach Southampton,
than as we leave it. As we leave it, the avenue ends abruptly in a naked country; but as
we turned round, and viewed it in retrospect,
it united with the woody scene around it,
which had a good effect. A retrospect also

afforded

afforded beautiful views over Southampton river, and its appendages, the town, New-foreſt, and the Iſle of Wight. All this pleaſing country appeared under various forms; and was often ſet off with good foregrounds.

Having paſſed the avenue, and a few miles of miſcellaneous country, no way intereſting, we entered, about the ſixth ſtone, a foreſt-ſcene, abounding with all the charms of that ſpecies of landſcape. In this we continued three or four miles.

From theſe woody ſcenes the country becomes more heathy ; but is ſtill diverſified with wood, and affords many pleaſing diſtances on the right ; till at length it ſuddenly degenerates into chalky grounds, which are of the ſame kind as thoſe deſcribed in our approach to Wincheſter *.

We left Wincheſter by the Baſingſtoke road; which paſſes through a country, with little picturefque beauty on either hand. It becomes by degrees flat and unpleaſant, and ſoon degenerates into common-field land, which, with its

* See page 44.

A A   ſtriped

ſtriped diviſions, is of all kinds of country generally the moſt unpleaſant.

Near Baſingſtoke ſtand the ruins of Baſing-houſe, which we cannot paſs without feeling a reſpeſt for the gallant figure it made, beyond that of any fortreſs of its ſize, in the civil wars of Charles I. It was at that time the ſeat of the Marquis of Wincheſter, who fortified and held it for the king, during the greateſt part of thoſe troubleſome times, though it underwent an almoſt continued blockade. Once it was ſo far reduced by famine, as to be on the point of ſurrendering ; and its relief by Colonel Gage was conſidered as one of the moſt ſol-dierly aſtions of the war. Lord Clarendon has detailed this gallant enterprize at length. The outlines of it are theſe. The King was then at Oxford. He had been applied to for aſſiſtance by the garriſon at Baſing-houſe ; but it was blockaded by ſo large a force, that all the mili-tary men about him thought any attempt to relieve it, deſperate. Gage, however, offered his ſervice ; and getting together a few volun-teers, well mounted, undertook the buſineſs. On Monday night he left Oxford, which is forty miles from Baſing-houſe ; came up with the beſiegers before da·light on Wedneſday

morn-

morning; forced their lines by an unexpected
attack; and entered the place with a ftring of
horfes laden with provifion. The enemy foon
found how contemptible a number had alarmed
them; and returning to their pofts, began to
clofe up the avenues. Gage, with that readi-
nefs of invention which is able to command
the crifis of a great action, fent orders into the
country, to provide quantities of provifion for
a large reinforcement, which he hourly expected. This intelligence gave a momentary
paufe to the motions of the enemy. A moment was all that Gage wanted. He iffued inftantly from the garrifon with his fmall troop
of horfe; and through bye roads got fafe to
Oxford without interruption. Thus relieved,
Bafing-houfe continued to baffle all the attempts of the Parliament, till the fatal battle of
Nafeby. After that event misfortunes came in
with a full tide upon the king. Every day
brought him fome new account of the lofs of
his garrifons; and among other places he had
the mortification to hear of the lofs of Bafing-
houfe. Cromwell himfelf appeared before it,
and fummoning it in haughty language, was
anfwered with fcorn. The incenfed chief fell
upon it with a body of his veteran troops; car-

ried

ried it by affault; and put the garrifon to the
fword.—Among the few fugitives that efcaped,
was the celebrated engraver Hollar, who had
been fhut up in the caftle. This event, in a
picturefque work, is a circumftance worth
mentioning.

From Bafingftoke we continued our route
to Bagfhot. Lord Albermarle's houfe and improvements appeared to great advantage, contrafted by the heath, which furrounded them.
They feemed like an ifland in the main. As
we approached Stains, the Duke of Cumberland's plantations in Windfor-park made a noble appearance.

From Stains we croffed the Thames at Kingfton, where we entered Surrey.

APPENDIX.

SINCE this volume went to prefs, Sir Jofhua Reynolds's Lectures fell into the author's hands, which he had never feen before. As they point out two or three miftakes which he had made, he thinks it proper to mention them in an Appendix. In page 46, fpeaking of monuments in churches, he expreffes his doubts, whether the " introduction of·them will be any " advantage to St. Paul's ; which the judicious " architect, he fuppofes, had already adorned " as much as he thought confiftent with the " fublimity of his idea." In fpeaking on the fame fubject, Sir Jofhua, on the contrary, informs us, that " Sir Chriftopher Wren left niches " in St. Paul's on purpofe for monuments, bufts, " fingle figures, bas-reliefs, and groups of " figures." Vol. ii. p. 242. The author can only fay, that he does not remember any niches or receffes in St. Paul's, which gave him ideas of this kind; but as what Sir Jofhua fays is given as *information*; and his remark depends only on *fuppofition*, and *recollection*, it muft of courfe give way.

In page· 112, he fpeak highly of Vandyck's fuperiority as a *portrait painter*; but flightly of

2   his

his abilities *in hiftory*. A large piece, in which Vandyck has many figures to manage, he fuppofes to be a work which required more fkill in compofition than Vandyck poffeffed. His opinion is formed chiefly on the great family-picture at Wilton, which gave occafion to thefe remarks; and on two large pictures which he had formerly feen, and examined at Houghton-hall; in none of which the compofition *pleafed him*. But Sir Jofhua Reynolds, in his Travels through Flanders, tells us, that he faw at Mecklin, a picture of the Crucifixion by Vandyck, which he thought one of the firft pictures in the world; and fcruples not to fay, he thinks Vandyck had a genius for hiftory-painting. The author cannot withftand fuch authority; but muft withdraw his own opinion—or, at leaft, keep it modeftly to himfelf.

But though he had the mortification to find he differed from Sir Jofhua Reynolds in thefe, and a few more particulars, he had the pleafure to find they agreed in a number of others. Two or three of them belong to the volume before us. In page 117, the author obferves that he had oftener than once judged falfely on the *firft fight* of Salvator's pictures, which pleafed him more on a fecond view. This, however, he confiders as a fault; for we expect from a good picture,

picture, as from a good man, a favourable impreffion at fight. Sir Jofhua's opinion of a good picture is the fame. He fays, " it fhould " pleafe at firft fight, and appear to incite the " fpectator's attention." Vol. i. p. 208.

In the 21ft page, the beautiful effect of eafy action in a ftatue, in oppofition to none at all, is confidered ; and the Venus, the Apollo, the liftening Slave, and the Farnefian Hercules refting from one of his labours, are inftanced. All thefe gentle modes of *action*, or *expreffion*, are confidered, in the paffage alluded to, as much more beautiful than the uninterefting vacancy of a conful ftanding erect in his robes.—He had the pleafure to fee remarks exactly fimilar to thefe in one of Sir Jofhua's Lectures (vol. i. p. 259.). " Thofe works of the ancients," fays he, " which are in the higheft efteem, have fome- " thing befide mere fimplicity to recommend " them. The Apollo, the Venus, the Lao- " coon, the Gladiator, have a certain compo- " fition of action, with contrafts fufficient to " give grace and energy in a high degree. But " it muft be confeffed of the many thoufand " ftatues which we have, their general charac- " teriftic is bordering at leaft on inanimate in- " fipidity."

THE END.

The Antique Map ~ Bookshop
Puddletown,
March 1994 £10